U.S. Marines in Action

U.S. Marines in Action

Tales of the Old Corps, 1773-1953

T. R. Fehrenbach

OPEN ROAD
INTEGRATED MEDIA
NEW YORK

All rights reserved, including without limitation the right to reproduce this book or any portion thereof in any form or by any means, whether electronic or mechanical, now known or hereinafter invented, without the express written permission of the publisher.

Copyright © 1962 by T. R. Fehrenbach

ISBN 978-1-4976-4021-4

This edition published in 2014 by Open Road Integrated Media, Inc.
345 Hudson Street
New York, NY 10014
www.openroadmedia.com

The author wishes to express his grateful appreciation for help rendered by:
Lt. Col. William J. Zaro, USMC.
Capt. Harvey B. Mayberry, USMCR.

Table of Contents

Part One
The Old Corps

One—The Age of Sail: 1775-1898   3
Two—Birth of a Mission:
   Guantanamo Bay, 1898   25
Three—Instrument of Policy:
   Haiti 1915-19   34
Four—Forces in Being:
   Belleau Wood 1918   46
Five—Proving Ground:
   Nicaragua 1927   66

Part Two
The Greatest Test

Six—Dark Island:
   Guadalcanal 1942   81
Seven—Bitter Lesson: Tarawa 1943   94
Eight—Banzai: Saipan 1944   109
Nine—Inevitable Encounter:
   Iwo Jima, 1945   117
Ten—The Last Island:
   Okinawa 1945   136

Part Three
A Newer Breed

Eleven—Bloody Rice: No Name Ridge 1950	155
Twelve—The Savage Land: Crisis at Yudam-ni 1950	168
Thirteen—Death on the Ridges: Toktong Pass 1950	179
Fourteen—Outpost: Reno, 1952	188

Foreword

This book does not purport to be a history of the United States Marine Corps, which has served in twelve major wars and more than two hundred lesser actions.

It is, instead, the record of certain significant Marine actions which illustrate Marine history as a whole. These incidents and battles do not have significance for Marines alone, but for all Americans.

They are part of our own history, our national story. However, they have largely been forgotten, because Americans have an imperfect sense of our past.

The men in these pages run curiously to type, as that splendid communicator on U.S. Marines, Colonel Thomason wrote. Most of them are professional soldiers; many are of that ubiquitous type without which no standing military body can exist: the professional private.

The gallantry of Marine officers is well-documented. The efficiency of Marine NCOs is indisputable. But still, without the professional private there would be no Marine Corps. He is the man who gets and does the dirty jobs. He is the man who carries them through, without much pay, with little recognition.

He is the Marine who sweats on the rifle range while the drums are silent, and the fires of patriotism not yet lit. He is not the gallant volunteer who rushes into the grandeur and tragedy of war, then, when the war is done, says to hell with it till next time.

He knows, as surely as the sun must rise, there will be a next time, and he prepares for it.

He likes the comradeship of the men around him; he likes the close-knit, parochial community of arms. If war is his occupation, the service is his home. Above all else, the most important thing in his life is the Corps. The Corps gives his life meaning; in return, he gives it his life. And it is a fact that many men, reservists and sometimes Marines, find their service as the defining moment of their lives. Once a Marine, always a Marine.

The men in these pages generally are not imaginative, nor are they sensitive to all the currents around them. Political correctness passed them by. Those who constantly visualize their own blood staining the earth rarely become professional soldiers. Since war is their occupation, most of these men do not much wonder at the tasks they are asked to do. They do not muse over the metaphysical or the meaning of it all, nor does combat come to them as a shock. Their eye on the enemy, until he is proven dead.

When this book was researched most of the Marines depicted in these actions were still living. Most — this was a different age and culture — for various reasons had no wish to be named. Therefore many names were changed. For example, the man identified as Corporal Cherry Reed in the Okinawa action, was the Honorable Blair "Bruzzy" Reeves, last Justice of the Texas Court of Appeals. When the book was first printed, he was entering on his political career and asked me to change his name, so that no one might think he was trading on his heroism. <u>Autre temps, autre moeurs.</u>

In the Old Corps few men got medals for doing their job — unlike today, when a soldier who has never heard a shot fired in anger may sprout rows of ribbons.

The names of officers, company commanders and above, which are recorded in history, have not been changed.

Few of these men are now alive. However, Lieutenant Colonel Ray Davis, now General, USMC-retired, was still erect and hearty when I saw him at the proceedings of the United States Naval Institute where I spoke in March, 1999.

Yet, the breed survives. Old and new, the country and the Corps have always needed this breed of man throughout our past.

We shall need him again.

T.R.F.
June, 1999

Part One

The Old Corps

The story of the first century of the United States Marines is as much composed of legend as of fact. To say this is to do the Corps no disservice, for legend is as important to a fighting organization as ever any fact. Legend, intertwined with solid fact to give it body, lends *mystique* to what is really a hard, dirty, monotonous trade, having occasional periods of great danger and excitement.

And *mystique* is as necessary to the men who live that hard, monotonous existence as the bread they eat, and the flag for which they are willing to die. No fighting unit which has made its mark upon the globe has ever been wholly without it.

Men do not live by bread alone, nor do they die willingly for purely rational reasons. Legends give them a code to live by, a standard to measure up to. And when there is a solid measure of truth to legend, each man who becomes a part of that legend may feel a certain pride that he belongs.

In battle — however odd this may seem to those who have never thrilled to the notes of *Retreat* or to the tales, oft recounted, of brave men's deeds — such pride pays off. No man wishes to mar the legend nor sully the great tradition, no matter how pressing his fear.

In its first hundred and twenty-five years, the Marine Corps was building tradition, its own *mystique*. While its story then is essentially the story of the Navy, an important groundwork was being laid.

In the age of sail, the Marines Corps had no chance to act as a fighting force of national significance. But it was laying in a store of brave men's deeds. . . .

One

The Age of Sail: 1775-1898

"You think this is bad, laddie? You should have been in the Old Corps!" Legendary remark made by the first United States Marine on the U.S.S. Alfred, Philadelphia Harbor, December, 1775, to the second Marine reporting aboard.

On the 10th day of November, 1775, the Continental Congress of the rebellious American colonies, assembled in Philadelphia, passed a resolution:

> That two battalions of Marines be raised consisting of one colonel, two lieutenant colonels, two majors, and other officers, as usual in other regiments; that they consist of an equal number of privates with other battalions; that particular care be taken that no persons be appointed to offices or enlisted into said battalions but such are good seamen or so acquainted with maritime affairs as to be able to serve with advantage by sea when required; that they be enlisted and commissioned to serve for and during the present war between Great Britain and the colonies, unless dismissed by order of Congress; that they be distinguished by the names of the First and Second Battalions of American Marines.

Using this resolution as a basis, Marine historians date the birth of the United States Marine Corps from November 10, 1775, some months before the said United States declared itself a nation.

However, as with many a resolution of that and later congresses, there is no evidence that it was ever implemented. Certainly, no

Marine officer achieved the rank of colonel during the Revolutionary War, and there is no evidence to suggest that any unit so large as a Marine regiment was ever recruited.

Part of the reason lies not in the ineptitude of the government of the emerging United States, but in the function of Marines themselves in those years.

In the age of sail, ships of war needed an additional complement above the sailing crew to perform certain functions requiring specific training. The sailors themselves had their hands full handling the ship, and later, manning the cannon. Men were needed to fight on deck to repel boarders, to place well-aimed musket fire on enemy vessels lying alongside, and to guard watering and forage parties sent ashore on hostile coasts. In addition, sea-going men trained in arms were sometimes needed on board for disciplinary reasons — pressed crews were not always reliable.

Sailing ships themselves required no fuel to span the world, and little maintenance for extended periods of time. They needed a quiet bay to careen, a place to lay aboard fresh water and sometimes fresh foods. Beyond that, they needed no foreign bases or support, and could remain at sea for years.

Sailing navies never contemplated extended action on land, for there were no reasons, military or logistical, for such actions. Consequently, ships' complements of sea-going soldiers were small, rarely larger than a company of one hundred men. And Marines, as they came to be called, were normally recruited for service in a single ship, as the sailing crew itself.

The history of modern Marines began with the formation in England in 1664 of the Duke of York and Albany's Maritime Regiment of Foot. This regiment served aboard ships of the Royal Navy, and its officers came to hold the King's Commission as a regular component of the British armed forces.

It was natural that the rebellious colonies should continue a system well-established by the mother country. With or without the action of the Continental Congress, Marines were recruited for each war ship, State or Continental, which went down the ways during the Revolutionary War.

After passing the resolution establishing Marines, the Congress gave a Philadelphian named Samuel Nicholas a commission as captain. Since Mr. Nicholas' best-known qualification in 1775 was as a frequenter of fashionable Philadelphia clubs and his uncle was Mayor, political influence may be suspected in the appointment. Yet the choice of what was to be the first Marine commandant was not a bad one.

Shortly, Captain Nicholas was joined in the exclusive circle of Marine officerdom, now numbering two, by one Robert Mullan. The reason for Captain Mullan's selection is clear — he owned Tun Tavern, a well-known hangout for seamen, and he soon proved himself a prodigious recruiter of men for the new service.

"Have you a rifle? How well can you shoot it?" Mullan liked to ask his customers. Getting the answer he liked, the grog would flow, along with talk of booty, bounty, and glory. No doubt, many a stout-hearted lad woke up the next morning wondering just what he had let himself in for.

The system worked so well that by February, 1776, when an American naval expedition to the Bahama Islands was ready to sail under Commodore Ezek Hopkins, Mullan had provided a force of 268 Marines to sail with it. Captain Nicholas boarded the flagship, *Alfred*, in command of its Marine company, while Mullan took command of the detachment aboard the *Columbus*.

Marines were essential, since the mission of the fleet was to capture a great store of British powder and shot believed to be stored on New Providence.

The landings at New Providence, while often billed as the first amphibious assault of the U. S. Navy and Marine Corps, were something less than a screaming success. Because of inept sailing on approach to the island, the element of surprise was lost. Then, sailing east from the harbor of Nassau with its forts, the fleet put Captain Nicholas ashore on a deserted stretch of beach with a party of 220 Marines and 50 seamen.

Safely ashore, Nicholas sent a message to the British governor of the island that all he wanted was the military stores, and that he would respect all private property. Having delivered this ultimatum he marched against Fort Montague, which guarded the harbor of Nassau to the east. More as a matter of good form than anything else, the weak British garrison fired three rounds from a 12-pounder, destroyed their cannon and withdrew.

A search of Fort Montague revealed no powder and shot, nor any other munitions. Since it was near dark, Nicholas decided to bed down for the night, then tackle Fort Nassau to the west in the morning.

The next day the governor surrendered Fort Nassau and the town of Nassau willingly. Warned by Nicholas' dispatch, he had loaded 150 barrels of gunpowder — desperately needed by the Continentals — onto a small vessel and slipped it out of the harbor around 3:00 A.M.

The gunpowder reached British garrisons in North America safely, and was happily employed by them against the rebels. Captain Nicholas, now a wiser man, realized that courtesy in time of war could be overdone.

He returned with the fleet to Philadelphia, and again he and Mullan recruited a new battalion — the old one had been rather depleted by the fact that colonials of the time never saw any reason to stick around once the action got a little dull. But since Washington and the Continental Army — the regulars — were desperate for men, this battalion did not go to sea. It was dispatched to Washington's Continental Line, thus early establishing what later became a regular affair in the lives of Marines.

The battalion fought at Trenton, and in the brilliant success at Princeton. Then, after a miserable winter at Morristown, where winter quarters were along the lines of the more famous Valley Forge, the battalion was split up and went back to sea. In 1777 Nicholas was made a major, and became undisputed Commandant of Marines.

Nicholas was not to fight again, but he did perform important duties for the new nation — including the personal escort of one million dollars in silver from Boston to Philadelphia through a countryside beset by British soldiers and unpaid colonial militia.

In 1779, the British erected a naval station at the mouth of the Penobscot River, in what is now Maine, much to the annoyance of the State of Massachusetts. Without asking help from the Continental Government, Massachusetts raised 16 ships of war and fifteen hundred militia and sent them north under command of Commodore Saltonstall, in the *Warren* which mounted 32 guns. With the expedition went 300 Marines.

On July 28th, the ground forces landed on the shores of Penobscot Bay, nine miles in from the Atlantic. General Lovell, the militia commander, emplaced a battery and began to make brave noises at the enemy fortifications.

Having only a few hundred men, the British commander, McLean, figured the jig was up.

Instead, the militia leaders staged a two-week town meeting, debating the best way to attack, while the single captain of Marines begged for orders to fight. While the meeting raged, Sir George Collier and a considerable British naval force reached Penobscot.

Whatever Commodore Staltonstall was, he was no John Paul Jones. Panicking, he fled for open water and Collier defeated him in detail, ship by ship. With all American ships sunk, run aground, or fleeing for home, the Marine detachment was left ashore in an unfriendly wilderness.

They went home on foot, covering 300 miles. For many years Marine standards bore the legend: *By Land, By Sea;* this is undoubtedly, however, not a referral to the above disaster, to which Marine courage contributed the one bright spot.

Marines fought also at Charlestown, South Carolina in 1780. The fiasco there cannot be laid at their door but again to militia leadership. After 1780, Marines took no further part in land action in the war.

But each American ship that put to sea carried its Marine complement, and in each naval action, Marines behaved with great gallantry. This story, however, properly belongs to the Navy.

Perhaps because they had been intended to be armed with rifles, and green was the traditional color worn by rifle units, orders during the Revolutionary War set forth forest green shirts and coats as Marine uniforms. However, since Congress inconsiderately forgot to appropriate money for both the rifles and uniforms, Marines often carried muskets and wore anything they could get their hands on. The Marine detachment aboard John Paul Jones' *Bon Homme Richard* is said to have confused things by wearing captured red coats.

The *Bon Homme Richard,* with 42 guns, engaged H. M. Frigate *Serapis,* mounting 50 guns, off Flaborough Head September 21, 1779, in the dusk. During one of the most savage ship-to-ship actions in naval history, Marine riflemen in the tops decimated the English officers and ratings aboard *Serapis,* aiming by moonlight. As *Bon Homme Richard's* gun decks were smashed by cannon shot, at one period in the battle only American marksmanship held the British boarders at bay.

The battle was decided by an American who crawled out on the main yard of *Bon Homme Richard* with a bucket of hand grenades. He hurled one through the main hatch of *Serapis*, into the gun-room below. Stored powder ignited, killing and wounding 38 crewmen. There is evidence to indicate this American was a Marine. After 3 hours and 30 minutes of firing, the *Serapis* struck, and the infant United States had won one of its most glorious battles at sea.

The war ended in 1783 with the independence of the new nation assured. With the end of danger, Congress showed its own independence by disbanding the Navy. The American Fleet's last ship, *Alliance*, was finally presented to the French Navy, officially as a token of friendship, but more likely as an economy measure.

With the complete disappearance of the Continental Navy in 1784, the Marines ceased to exist.

Not until May 1, 1798, due to troubles with this same France, was the Navy Department reestablished. A few months later, legislation set up a United States Marine Corps, and President Adams appointed William W. Burrows Major and Commandant.

As authorized, the Marine Corps was still hardly a force to frighten the great powers of the world. The Table of Organization called for 1 major, 4 captains, 28 lieutenants, and 848 enlisted men of all grades, including 32 fifers and drummers.

Moving to Philadelphia, still the capital of the United States, Burrows was able to lobby a promotion to lieutenant colonel, at which rank the Commandancy stood for many years. The total strength of the Corps, also, would stand at 1,000 or less for many decades.

In 1801, when the Pasha of Tripoli declared war on the United States, due to its failure to bargain collectively at the tribute table, the Corps numbered under 500 officers and men, which makes it rather amazing that the second line to the Marine Hymn ever came to be written.

The Navy scraped together some ten warships and sent them to the Mediterranean where they sank a few Tripolitanian vessels and tried to blockade the coast — a job too big for the size of the force. With the war in a sort of unhappy stalemate, a man named William Eaton approached the American government with a scheme for ending it.

Eaton, sometime captain in the Revolutionary Army, had been United States Consul at Tunis, a neighboring Barbary State to Tripoli.

He knew a great deal of the internal affairs of Tripoli, including the fact that the Pasha, Yusuf Karamanli, in order to get the throne, had exiled one older brother and murdered another. Eaton figured that if the exiled brother, Hamid Karamanli, could be returned to Tripoli with U.S. backing, the resulting civil war would make Tripoli easy pickings for the Navy.

Eaton was able to sell this plan to the President, and he appeared off the Barbary Coast in 1804.

Last word of Hamid had come from Egypt, and Eaton collected an escort of seven United States Marines from the fleet, and a good-looking young Marine lieutenant named Presley O'Bannon; with this party he proceded to the Nile. In time, he located Hamid, languishing in exile with an entourage of ninety servants, including Arab bodyguards and his harem.

Hamid did not prove particularly eager to set out on any such wild adventure as the *ferenghi* proposed; life was much too comfortable along the Nile. Only after Eaton and O'Bannon had scoured the Alexandria waterfront, corraling some thirty-eight Greek adventurers and procured two cannon, did he show interest. Reluctantly, he agreed to march across the desert to the east to Derna, Tripoli's second city, some six hundred miles away.

Eaton hired camels and drivers to transport Hamid's entourage, and he appointed himself General of the Revolutionary Army of Tripoli. Then, he ordered the march on Derna, beginning the most fantastic episode in Marine history.

Something of Eaton's and O'Bannon's persuasive powers can be told from the fact that the revolutionary army finally arrived on the Tripolitanian coast. Several times the camel drivers struck for higher wages. Hamid developed progressively colder feet as Derna grew closer. The Greek mercenaries, who didn't care whom they fought, several times engaged in private war with Hamid's Arab guards.

But reach the coast they did, and there supplies from the fleet arrived just in time.

But there was now another problem — the public seemed completely indifferent to the fact that Hamid had returned, and the governor of Derna remained loyal to Yusuf. The revolutionary army still consisted of General Eaton, Lieutenant O'Bannon, seven Marines, and less than a hundred Greek and Arab mercenaries.

O'Bannon, who was nothing if not high-spirited, was all for attacking. Leaving Hamid to watch, he led an assault on Derna, supported by naval gunfire from the fleet offshore. Incredibly, he broke into the populous city and his motley army captured the arsenal.

O'Bannon, as the only American officer present, broke out the United States flag and raised it over the city. Then, his seven Marines wheeled a couple of cannon around toward the governor's palace and let fly.

The governor decided to retire; these foreigners showed too damned much energy in the desert heat. Suddenly, everybody in Derna was for Hamid Karamanli, and the revolutionary army was a going concern.

Recruiting a strong force from the populace, Eaton and O'Bannon met and turned back a numerous expedition Pasha Yusuf sent against them.

William Eaton, who had put up most of the money for his expedition out of his own pocket, began to see a happy end to his efforts. The civil war looked like a success. Yusuf seemed to be hanging on the ropes, and Eaton prepared to march on the city of Tripoli.

But now Eaton and O'Bannon were to be taken in the rear, in one of the most famous doublecrosses in history. After Eaton had departed, President Jefferson reviewed his scheme and, rather understandably, decided he had been sold a bill of goods. The President, hearing no word from North Africa, decided further to send one Tobias Lear as a plenipotentiary to treat with Pasha Yusuf.

It was a sorry choice.

Tobias Lear listened to Yusuf's protestations about the trouble the Americans had caused and sympathetically agreed this was unwarranted interference. Furthermore, Barbary pirates had always made a living by exacting tribute, about the only means open to an underdeveloped nation before the days of foreign aid, and Tobias Lear agreed on the principle of the thing.

When Yusuf and Lear had talked enough, the United States had agreed to give in on almost every point that had caused the war in the beginning.

Eaton had made promises to Hamid and his followers — promises he thought would be supported by the United States. Now, he suddenly received orders from Commodore Barron of the Mediterranean

Fleet to return Derna to Yusuf, and to evacuate Hamid and certain selected followers.

There was nothing to be done about it. Hamid and the valiant Greeks were taken aboard ship for refuge in Malta. Hamid's Arab supporters were left behind, and there is no record as to whether Yusuf employed flaying alive, boiling in oil, or the bastinado as their reward.

Hamid, used to African politics, was sportsmanlike about the whole thing. He presented O'Bannon with his own curved scimitar, and thereby started a tradition in the Corps, which wears a curved sword to this day.

Eaton returned to the States, trying at least to recover the funds he had spent from his own pocket. After some years of lobbying and watching his bill die in committee, he was finally granted a year's pay in the rank of captain, his old Army grade.

O'Bannon, the only Marine officer ever to take a hostile stronghold and to raise the American flag over a captured fort, got nothing for his trouble, the government figuring these acts were somewhat too irregular to be rewarded by promotion.

Presley O'Bannon is reported to have told them what part of his anatomy they could kiss. He resigned and moved West where presumably his abilities found ample reward.

While the War with Tripoli was being won on the battlefield and lost at the peace table, Commandant Burrows had realized that the Corps was a very small service, and seemingly not apt to get larger, unless something could be done.

In one way, the Marines were in a unique position — they were the only military force garrisoned in the new capital of Washington, D. C. He decided that it would be a good thing to have something to show the Old Man — in this case, the President of the United States. He also decided he could get quite a bit of mileage out of a band to serenade the President and government officials.

Burrows, an energetic leader, was not stopped by the fact there was no authorization or money for a Marine Band. He whipped off a letter to each officer of the Corps, setting up a table by rank of the amount each was to contribute out of his pocket each month toward such a band.

The instruments paid for and the bandsmen trained, on New Year's Day Burrows led the band to the Presidential Mansion and blazed away. Everyone, except a few soreheads drawing $25 a month lieutenant's pay, was delighted.

Quickly, Marine concerts at the White House became an institution, and a new tradition was formed. Later bandleaders of merit, such as John Philip Sousa, helped make this band into the cherished organization it is today.

For the record, the Marine Band has not been supported by "voluntary" contributions for some time.

The War of 1812 found the nation with almost no fighting forces, as usual, but the Navy had received fortunate experience in the actions against France in 1798 and the Barbary War. Heavily outnumbered, it still wrote several pages of glory in action against the massive British fleet. In all these actions Marines served with gallantry, but again this story is that of the Navy, for the Marines fought as ship's complements.

Marines also fought at Bladensburg, and with General Jackson at New Orleans. Though they acquitted themselves well, they were too few to affect the outcome of either battle.

Following the War of 1812, due to the rather poor quality of the appointed commandants and the attitude toward armed forces in general in the country, the Marine Corps had sunk into a state of apathy, along with the Regular Army and Navy.

It took the "Age of Henderson" to pull the Corps out of it.

In 1820, at the age of 37, Major Archibald Henderson was promoted to fill the Corps' single lieutenant-colonelcy which went with the post of Commandant. He was a decorated veteran who had commanded the Marine contingent aboard the *Constitution,* and a man who had strong ideas of what a military force in general, and the Marine Corps in particular, should be.

Under Archibald Henderson, the Corps began to build a reputation. While its strength was only 50 officers and fewer than 900 men, Henderson knew that the backbone of any military organization was pride and training.

He took personal direction of every activity of the Corps. The strictest discipline was enforced, and Marines were continually trained in the latest developments in weapons and tactics. Since at this time, the Army actually had too few officer vacancies to accept the entire graduating class at West Point, Henderson snared as many of the good graduates as he could for the Marines.

The Marines became a hard service, but their quality improved.

For the first decade or so of Henderson's reign, there were no wars. However, as a federal force, the Corps took part in disaster operations and in quelling certain serious riots. Marine discipline became a byword across a basically undisciplined country.

Then, in 1836, Archibald Henderson closed the door of Marine Corps Headquarters in Washington and tacked this notice on it:

GONE TO FLORIDA TO FIGHT INDIANS. WILL BE BACK WHEN WAR IS OVER.

A. HENDERSON
COL. COMMANDANT

In 1819 Spain had sold Florida to the United States, neither party consulting the Seminole Indians who were the state's principal inhabitants. By 1834 the Seminoles had become a major nuisance to Americans trying to follow the sun, and the government resolved to remove them to Arkansas.

A number of Seminole chiefs were forced to sign the treaty of removal. One, a half-breed named Osceola, buried his hunting knife in the parchment when it was read to him, and shortly afterward showed other disturbing signs of non-conformity.

The Florida frontier settlements exploded in fire and death as the Seminoles took the warpath. Right was more on their side than on that of the government — but this could not be the concern of the small regular forces sent to quell them.

An Army detachment of 140 men led by Major Dade marched from Fort Brooke at the head of Tampa Bay against the Indians. Dade proceeded into the swamps accompanied by colors and field music, making a grand show to overawe the ignorant enemy. Major Dade had a lot to learn about fighting Indians. Unfortunately, he got no chance to learn.

At the Big Withlacoochee, the Army was ambushed by Seminoles and runaway slaves from Georgia. At the first volley from the tall grass Dade and half his men fell; the rest were massacred piecemeal by the not so ignorant savages. It was a disaster second only to Custer's debacle at the Little Big Horn. One private, wounded, fought his way to safety, only to die of his injuries after telling his story.

On the same day Major Dade was assuring his particular place in history, Osceola and a picked band of warriors crept close to a small house some two hundred yards beyond the gates of Fort King. Here

General Wiley Thompson, USA, and nine of his friends were dining, while discussing the stubbornness of Seminoles who did not realize that Arkansas was the land of opportunity.

The day was hot and after the bottle had been passed a couple of times, Thompson ordered the windows opened.

Before the jug could make another passage, the room was filled with howling savages and the crash of musketry. Thompson and four of his guests fell dead and were scalped while the remaining diners fled for their lives.

Osceola particularly relished taking Wiley Thompson's mutton chops, since he was President Jackson's personal emissary, with orders to oversee the Indians' removal.

Things were obviously out of hand.

The thousand regulars of the U.S. Army faced more than three thousand aroused Seminoles. The militia of the southern states proved absolutely worthless under the miserable conditions of the fighting in south Florida, and soon the Indians in Alabama and Georgia took the warpath, forcing their withdrawal.

Completely unable to cope with the uprising because of lack of men, President Jackson ordered the Marine Corps to have all available men report for service with the Army. Henderson tacked his notice on the door and moved south, stripping every Marine and Navy installation on the way. He reported to General Winfield Scott in Georgia with 38 officers and more than four hundred men.

The Marine contingent was brilliantly prepared for fighting in the Everglades. Discarding the green and white uniforms of the day, they appeared in pure white battle dress, a joy to Indian marksmen. Their weapons were largely smoothbore muskets, but a significant number of men were issued the new Colt rifles, which could be counted on for rapid fire — and also to blow up, once they got hot.

First they moved against the rebellious Creeks in Georgia, and by the end of the summer, that trouble was over. Then, they moved south against the Seminoles. By now, the Marines had grown into a six-company regiment, augmented by Army troops and friendly Creeks.

Immediately, their troubles began. Pushing on from a skirmish action at Wahoo Swamp, they drove the Indians back into Great Cypress Swamp. In every action, the Indians were routed — at least, when pressed, they melted away into the dense vegetation.

Occasionally the Marines killed or captured a squaw or a runaway Negro slave.

No victory could be won in the difficult terrain, but finally the Seminoles agreed to a truce. Henderson was recalled to Washington, and brevetted — which meant he got the rank but not the pay — of a brigadier general. Two companies of Marines were left in Florida. Due to action by the whites, the truce was promptly broken. The guerrilla war flared again. Four thousand Seminoles were rounded up and shipped to Arkansas, but the majority held out in the swamps. For five years Henderson tried to get his boys back from Florida duty, without success. The Army had them, and it wasn't about to let trained men go.

Serving with the so-called Mosquito Fleet, half of the Marines died of fever or disease.

After seven years, 1842, fighting gradually came to a halt. Nobody had won, and no peace was signed, but there was a general agreement that the whites and Indians would leave each other alone.

For the record books, it would be nice to be able to declare a Marine victory, but at last report the Seminoles are still holding out in the Everglades.

Henderson again turned his efforts to strengthening the Corps, and was able to get new authorizations for men and equipment. Marines, with the fleet, began to operate all over the world, wherever trouble threatened Americans or American interests. Many small, isolated actions were fought, against pirates, slave traders, and native rebellions.

In 1846, the United States went to war again, this time against Mexico. While the most significant result of Marine participation in this war was the acquisition of the first line to the Marine Hymn, some aspects of their actions are interesting.

The United States has received great abuse over the Mexican War, even from its own citizens. Certain facts are not evident to many latter-day historians: In the 1840's Mexico and the United States were not disparate in population; America was by no means industrial at the time; and the Mexican armed forces were — throughout the war — considerably larger than those fielded by the "Colossus of the North." Most European observers at the start of the war, including the veteran Duke of Wellington, if forced to choose, picked Mexico.

This is not to state the contest was wholly equal. The American generation raised on the "Middle Border" was beyond doubt the toughest this country has ever seen, and the war, at least in the southern tier of states, was entered upon with gusto. Americans of the Age of Manifest Destiny were encumbered by few moral doubts of the wisdom of their nation dominating the continent.

Mexico, a land which has consistently produced men of great bravery, was, at the time, an empire in the stages of dissolution. Covering vast areas, including thinly populated California, Arizona, and New Mexico, hampered by poor communications and miserable organization, the Mexican territories were about to separate of their own weight. Worse, Mexico had been and was to continue to be rocked by terrible internal strife between clericals and liberals, and beset by leaders lacking in ability of any kind, military or otherwise.

During 1835-1836 the Mexican province of Texas, inhabited mainly by immigrants of American stock, revolted and made it stick. After ten years as a republic, Texas entered the American Union, a fact regretted still by Mexico and some few diehard Texans. Two great empires met on the Rio Grande.

Both Mexico and Texas claimed the territory between the Nueces River in South Texas and the Rio Grande River. The old Spanish authorities themselves had been a little dubious as to which river constituted the boundaries of the Province of Texas, but inasmuch as no one lived in the disputed area, it had been a matter for the shrugging of shoulders.

Annexing Texas, the United States declared that whatever the Texans claimed in the way of boundaries was good enough for them, and regular troops were sent to the Rio Grande even while negotiations with Mexico were going on.

On the Rio Grande, General Zachary "Rough and Ready" Taylor built a fort in a bend of the river and, faced by a Mexican army three times his size keeping to the south of the disputed territory, he engaged each morning in raising the colors, to the accompaniment of much bugle blowing, beating of drums, and sounding of cannon.

Watching this display on territory they felt rightly belonged to them, the irritation of the Mexican soldiery is understandable. One day, after a particularly colorful display of military ceremony on the north side of the Rio Grande, somebody pulled a trigger on the south bank.

"American troops have been fired on, on American soil!" cried the President to Congress.

Congress, never one to buck the President when the chips are down, came through.

Zachary Taylor, making most of the tactical mistakes in the book, found himself waist-deep in Mexicans. He won two victories more by the fighting enthusiasm of his troops than by any genius on his part.

The best thing that can be said of American high leadership in the war is that the Mexican leadership gave them no real competition.

But Taylor on the Rio Grande, and the Navy lying off the Mexican coast, could not bring the war to a conclusion. An expeditionary force was raised to land at Vera Cruz and march inland to take the enemy capital, Mexico City.

Even Marines ignorant of history will know what action Brevet Brigadier Archibald Henderson took. He volunteered a regiment of Marines to go with Expedition Commander-in-Chief Winfield Scott.

However, due to reluctance of Navy commanders engaged in a shooting war to part with their shipboard detachments, a regiment could not be raised. Eventually a battalion, under Lieutenant Colonel Sam Watson, reported to Scott on July 16, 1847, and was attached to an Army Force headed by Brigadier Franklin Pierce. Unfortunately, the battalion was largely made up of new recruits, and as green as the enthusiastic Army volunteers.

Sam Watson himself had seen service in 1812, which made him a little overripe for service south of the border.

Heavily outnumbered and in the land of the enemy, Winfield Scott decided that, what Cortez had done three hundred years before, he could do, too. He left his shore base guarded by cripples, abandoned any attempt to keep a line of communications, and marched toward Mexico City.

When the great Wellington, who had marched inland on the Spanish Peninsula in the Napoleonic Wars, was told of this, he said, "Scott is lost."

Everybody but Scott agreed.

Scott fought his way to Mexico City while the Marine Battalion, much to its disgust, guarded the supply trains in the rear.

Outside the capital, the Army forces found their advance blocked by the great Citadel of Chapultepec, a formidable fortress on high ground.

Major General John Quitman's Army Division — in those days units took the names of their commanders rather than numerical designations — was ordered to attack to the south, General Gideon J. Pillow's Division to advance from the west.

Quitman formed special assault companies of 120 men, headed by picked officers. Major Twiggs of the Marine Battalion led one, and Marines and soldiers were intermingled freely in the assault parties.

In the early light of September 13, 1847, American artillery blasted the heights of Chapultepec in preparation for the attack. Mexican artillery replied so heavily that Quitman's forces were completely pinned down and unable to move.

Major Levi Twiggs, trying to get the attack to shove off, stood erect, yelling at his company to get moving. He was shot and killed instantly.

The other Marines, realizing that to stay under fire was worse than attacking, wanted to go forward. Colonel Watson refused to do this. As part of Pierce's Brigade, he held the Marine Battalion back until he had specific orders what to do.

Mexican field guns had been wheeled up to fire into the Marines, forcing them to seek cover in ditches alongside a road. Captain George Terrett, an experienced Marine officer, did not need orders to realize the artillery pieces had to be silenced. He was at the head of the Brigade column, and he ordered a frontal attack against the battery, while a platoon moved against the gunners' flank.

Seeing themselves surrounded by Marines moving up the deep ditches along the road, the Mexican artillerymen abandoned their guns.

At the head of the column, Terrett had not received Sam Watson's order to stand fast until the dust settled. He saw the foe in full retreat, and obeyed his instincts. With a total force of only forty-odd men, he pressed forward after the fleeing gunners.

Mexican cavalry charged him, and he used the captured guns just in time to break up the lancers' formations before he and his men were speared. With the cavalry unhorsed and scattered all over the terrain, he ordered the advance.

Moving far ahead of the main force, he ran into a series of Mexican entrenchments held by close to a thousand disorganized enemy troops. He immediately attacked.

The Mexicans knocked him back with a bloody nose, half his force killed or wounded. He attacked again, this time turning the enemy's flank. The Mexican officers, more confused as to the real situation than Terrett, who thought his own Brigade was behind him, took off, and their men followed.

Terrett now had less than twenty men. He found some stragglers from Army units and pressed them into his small force. With this tiny group, he was able to clear all the approaches to Mexico City.

Near San Cosme Gate he met a young lieutenant named Ulysses S. Grant and twenty-six Army regulars. Grant, much like Terrett, had gotten lost in the confusion. Joining forces, Army and Marines seized San Cosme Gate, figuring to hold it as an entrance to the city until the main body arrived.

Only, the main body was not coming. After an hour, word reached the first Americans in Mexico City to withdraw.

In tune with the free and easy ways of a gallant age, Terrett and his Marines accepted Lieutenant Grant's offer to remain with the 11th Infantry, United States Army. They never did get back to their parent battalion until after the campaign.

But in the meantime, Chapultepec had been reduced, and the American Army, which could have had the capital courtesy of Messers Terrett and Grant, was preparing to attack again the next day. And Major General Quitman, who had had a bad time before Chapultepec, was not happy with his new orders.

A volunteer general, Quitman figured the Regulars were getting to him, for Scott now ordered him only to make a diversionary threat against the city gates, while the Regular Army division commanded by Bill Worth actually took the city. And John Quitman was no man to take discrimination lying down. He decided not to wait for the regulars to hog the glory tomorrow.

Without a by-your-leave, he borrowed part of General Pillow's Division and took off for the city. He almost reached the gates before heavy Mexican gunfire stopped him. Meeting opposition from both front and flanks, Quitman ordered the charge, and four times personally led the assault. Whatever kind of soldier he was, John Quitman was hardly lacking in bravery.

Just short of nightfall, thirst, exhaustion, loss of men, and scarcity of ammunition forced Quitman to break off his attack a few yards short of the city gates and dig in.

The wild American charges, however, had had a poor effect on the nerves of the Mexican defenders, especially General Santa Anna. As soon as darkness fell, the Mexican commander withdrew his troops from the city, leaving it open to the invader.

In the dawn, John Quitman was kicking his boys awake, determined to have another go at taking Mexico City ahead of the Regular Army. Before his motley assortment of volunteers and Marines could get started, however, a solitary Mexican soldier came out of the gates with a white flag.

It was a ragtag but thoroughly dangerous mob that walked cautiously into the ancient capital of Montezuma. Quitman, fairly worn-out, his shoes missing, hobbled along at its head, collar open, sword in hand. Behind him came a bloody, dirty throng of Army regulars, state volunteers, and U.S. Marines.

The abandoned Mexican civilians, crossing themselves, scurried to hide their women and their silver.

Quitman barely had time to get his men to form ranks at the central plaza and to round up a few buglers and drummers to render Honors to the General by the time Winfield Scott arrived.

There is no official record of their opening conversation.

During the Mexican War, Marines also served off the coast of California, and took part in many raids on the Mexican coast. One Marine officer, a Lieutenant Archibald Gillespie, served as Military Governor of Los Angeles. This particular stewardship both the Angelenos and the Marines would prefer to forget, since Gillespie's peculiar talents for governing resulted in a general uprising against authority in Southern California.

In the years just before the Mexican War, the colors of the Corps carried the words: *To the Shores of Tripoli*, in memory of the superhuman efforts of O'Bannon and his seven men. Soon, in memory of George Terrett, the inscription was changed to read: *From the Shores of Tripoli to the Halls of the Montezumas*.

The name of the man who wrote the first verse of the Marine Hymn is not known. However, it was penned shortly after the action at San Cosme Gate, and it is obvious the author, after trying to set the above slogan to music, said to hell with historical accuracy and came up with the present version.

There is some doubt over where the music came from. An early Marine bandleader claimed the tune derived from Offenbach's comic opera *Genevieve de Brabant*. A band member with a Spanish wife said it was much more like an old Spanish drinking song. It was not made encumbent on any Marine to accept either version.

In the 1850's the Corps continued to serve on the seven seas, landing in Japan, Fiji, Latin America, and China. It now had a distinctive sword pattern after O'Bannon's presentation scimitar, and an inspiring hymn from the actions in Mexico. Far more important, it had a record of deeds of conspicuous gallantry, and the imprint of the firm hand of General Archibald Henderson.

On January 26, 1859, Henderson died in office at the age of seventy-six. His devotion to duty, discipline, and training, and his indelible effect on the Corps cannot be questioned. Such men are vitally important to the making of a military force — and after their deaths they even achieve a certain popularity.

But Henderson's long tenure, and the longevity system in effect in the Corps was beginning to have a serious side effect. Henderson was succeeded by Lieutenant Colonel John Harris, who was almost as old as Henderson, and who had been waiting for his eagles for forty-five years.

Promotion in all of the services in this period was fantastically slow, and as the smallest, the Corps suffered most. It took years for men to advance to corporal or sergeant, and the top enlisted grades were thoroughly grayheaded. Officers commonly stayed in the grade of lieutenant well into middle age, and the majority of field officers were too old for any kind of active duty.

Colonel Harris, on assuming the post of commandant, was more ready for pension than for the storm that was breaking upon the nation.

In 1859 the lines of coming conflict were drawing tight across a divided nation. A company of Marines under Lieutenant Israel Greene put down a rebellion by a fanatic named John Brown at Harper's Ferry, Virginia. Greene acted under the overall command of an Army lieutenant colonel, Robert E. Lee.

Within short months, neither Lee nor Greene were in the federal service. Resigning to join the Confederacy with them were the son of

Archibald Henderson, Major George Terrett of Mexico fame, and almost fifty per cent of the Corps' commissioned strength.

Both the nation and the Corps were to see their lowest years at this time.

Led by aging and enfeebled officers, and left out of the mainstream by government policy, the United States Marine Corps played no significant part in the American Civil War. Marine detachments served gallantly as part of ships' crews, but on the whole the war was not naval in nature.

Very early, Washington decided to fight the secession through the use of volunteer units. The Regular Army was not greatly expanded, but Army officers were sought for and received command of volunteer divisions and brigades raised by the states. Lieutenants fresh from West Point soon wore eagles and even stars. The regular Marines who stayed with the Union had no such opportunity.

Millions of volunteers donned blue or gray, but there was no provision for volunteers in forest green. Over-stocked with superannuated field officers, given no mission in the war, the Corps stagnated.

Colonel Harris died in 1864. Gideon Welles, Secretary of the Navy, knew something had to be done, and he took a drastic step toward the revitalization of the Corps — he appointed Major Jacob Zeilin, with only three seniority in grade, to the position of Commandant. Then, with approval from President Lincoln, all officers senior to Zeilin on the regular list were retired.

The story of these years is best told by a glance at the Marine Corps casualty list in the bloodiest war in American history: 77 killed in action, 257 dead from natural causes, 1,000 deserters.

Under Zeilin, the Corps began the long, painful struggle back, as it had in 1820 under young Archibald Henderson. It would take decades to complete the task.

By the close of its first century, the United States Marine Corps had had a long and rather colorful history, but it hadn't done anything really important.

After the Civil War, in the waning years of the nineteenth century, the very future of the Corps seemed in doubt. Strong opinion in both Army and Navy was ready to do away with an outfit which, while giving devoted service in most wars, hadn't done anything either the Army or the Navy couldn't do as well.

Quite a few Marines officers, decades in grade, might even have agreed. They might have done better on the Army or the Navy list.

For with the advent, in the 1800's, of steam-powered ships, the need for armed sea-going detachments began to disappear. The Navy felt that bluejackets could now take over such functions.

But even as sail disappeared — slowly, for naval men were as sentimental about sailing ships as old cavalrymen were about horses — a new factor in naval warfare was appearing. A modern fleet became bound to refueling bases as no old time armada had ever been. Steamships needed coal, and later, oil. A fleet must have advance bases in time of war, or it could not operate in unfriendly waters.

In the late 1800's the United States possessed almost no overseas bases, and it had few friends who could be relied on in case of trouble. In event of war, bases would have to be acquired the hard way.

Who would acquire them?

The Navy, said a large body of opinion, mostly in the Navy. Abolish the Marine Corps and expand the Navy so that it could seize and defend an advance base against an organized enemy.

But other opinion pointed out that this was a delicate maneuver, and that the Navy had no history of or skill in ground fighting. The Marine Corps, small as it was, was already a force in being, with valuable experience. The Corps, enlarged, should be given the mission.

The argument went on. It might still be going on if the Spanish-American War — and the United States Marines — had not resolved it.

On February 15, 1898, in the evening, the United States battleship *Maine* blew up at anchor in Havana harbor. Cubans as far away as eleven miles heard the explosion as the forward section of the *Maine* went up in flame. Captain Sigsbee, USN, stumbled from his cabin, bumped into his Marine orderly, Private William Anthony.

The young Marine came to attention, saluted and said: "Sir, I beg to report the Captain's ship is sinking."

Two hundred thirty-two sailors and twenty-eight Marines went to the bottom with *Maine*. Neither a United States Board of Inquiry nor investigations by the Spanish rulers of Cuba satisfactorily explained the cause of the disaster.

But the Spaniards, who were fighting a repressive colonial war in Cuba, were tried by the American press and found guilty. The tabloids and the public screamed for action. On April 19, 1898 Congress declared Cuba free of Spain and President McKinley was empowered to use troops to make it so.

Understandably, Spain declared war.

The United States was spoiling for a scrap — but as usual, it had very little to fight with. The Marine Corps Commandant, Colonel Heywood, was ordered to organize a force to fight in Cuba. He stripped every naval installation on the Atlantic coast and came up with a 647-man battalion under the command of Lieutenant Colonel Robert W. Huntington, a veteran of the Civil War.

Huntington's battalion sailed for Key West where it underwent arduous training. On June 10, 1898 it splashed ashore at Guantanamo Bay — the first United States troops to land in Cuba.

Two

Birth of a Mission: Guantanamo Bay, 1898

The Marines have landed and the situation is well in hand. From a dispatch filed by Richard Harding Davis, war correspondent.

From the hill overlooking Guantanamo Bay Lieutenant Colonel Robert W. Huntington could see a vast expanse of dense green foliage, rimmed by a vaster expanse of blue-green water. Far out on that water wisps of smoke coming from their stacks, rode the U.S.S. *Marblehead,* from which his battalion had debarked, and the U.S.S. *Dolphin,* standing by to give him naval gunfire support when he called for it.

But so far not a single gun had fired this 10th day of June, 1898. The only hostile action against the Marine battalion coming ashore had been launched by mosquitoes.

Huntington slapped at his sweaty face, cursing as his full beard scratched his irritated neck. He had done this sort of thing before, but it had been a long time since '65.

He eyed the thick tropical growth that grew almost to the water's edge again. Hell, there were Spaniards about. From the Cuban *insurrectos'* reports the staff had estimated there were at least 9,000 enemy troops — both Spanish regulars and Cuban loyalists. Against this force he had brought ashore five infantry companies and a battery of four 3-inch quickfirers, all regular Marines. The best part of the whole damned Marine Corps, in fact — and Huntington, a supremely confident man, figured this made the odds close to even.

Still, it was an unwholesome feeling, being the first Americans to set foot in Cuba. Nobody knew what to expect, least of all Huntington. This was something new, this seizing a harbor in enemy territory. So far as Huntington knew, it hadn't been done before. But it had to be done if Admiral Sampson were to keep up his blockade of the Spanish Fleet, holed up forty miles to the west in Santiago harbor.

Sampson had to recoal and if his squadrons steamed back to the States to coaling stations, Cervera could easily escape. Nobody wanted the Spanish fleet on the high seas — not with the American Expeditionary Force readying in Florida for a landing on the island.

Huntington's orders were to land and secure Guantanamo Bay. Secured, the Atlantic Fleet could use it as an advance base of operations. Well, Huntington had landed, but he could not report Guantanamo secured. Not yet.

All day his men had dragged their equipment over the broiling beaches and up on the high ground. They had ammunition, rations, tents and the 3-inchers ashore now. Below him Colonel Huntington watched a small party of men from C and D Companies sweating more crates up from the beach. They had their shirts off and they looked more like a pack of stevedores than Marines.

Well, that was all right. If they were going to serve in the tropics, those bloody idiots in the quartermaster corps were going to have to come up with something besides blue woolen uniforms. Huntington was conscious of the sodden feel of his hot tunic under his beard.

Frowning, Huntington watched the battalion perimeter being laid out. Privates Snavely and Jester were clearing rifle pits behind some fallen logs. He knew Snavely, a big blue-eyed Ohioan with corn-silk moustaches. Snavely, large and methodical, was a professional private — the type without which no professional military force could exist. Jester, little and dark and baldheaded, was the same. Ordinary men, not too imaginative. A damn far cry from those wild-eyed amateurs that New York fellow, Roosevelt, had formed out in Texas.

He saw Sergeant Quick stop beside the laboring privates and murmur a quiet word. A stolid man, John H. Quick, but an NCO to be relied on. He wished he could say the same for that correspondent fellow, Stephen Crane. Huntington wanted no part of a correspondent with his force, but he couldn't antagonize the press.

Captain Elliott, his face tanned, his eyes cool over his dark lip hair, was reporting the camp pitched and secure. It was almost dusk, the day fading in a flaring, red tropical twilight.

"Very good, Captain," Huntington said. "We'll wait for them to open the ball."

And shortly after good dark, the ball opened. The first warning was a rattle of rifle shots against the outposts which Huntington had carefully spotted about the camp. Two of the pickets fell dead.

Angrily the battalion stood to, fingering rifles, fixing long bayonets. But there was no attack, only a desultory firing. Several times Marines thought they saw the enemy in the dark brush and returned the fire. Mocking yells drifted back to them.

Willis Snavely, lying in his damp rifle pit behind a palm log, didn't like the sound of it. In the first place, he didn't like this night fighting. Civilized troops, by God, fought during daylight, then got their rest by dark. But you couldn't expect these Spicks to fight properly. He touched the bolt of his Krag and felt reassured. A good man could get off better than a dozen aimed shots a minute with these new repeating rifles — if he had something to aim at.

Behind him he heard Sergeant Quick say calmly, "Don't shoot until the word is passed."

Then at 1 A.M., screaming and yelling, the enemy came out of the jungle. Snavely saw the long, probing orange streaks of rifle fire, and he saw dark forms plunging up the hill, starlight gleaming from honed machete blades.

An officer yelled something, and Sergeant Quick said, "Fire at will!"

They were coming from both sides. Then the Marine perimeter vomited flame and lead, and the attack melted away. This time there were no mocking calls from the jungle.

Now the enemy began firing wildly from the brush surrounding the Marine battalion. Bullets sang overhead, clipped through the logs, scattered sand and dirt. Snavely fired twice, three times, at the flashes, feeling a touch of fear. By God, you couldn't see anything. You couldn't tell what the hell was going on!

"Stand fast — stand fast!" That was Quick's voice steady and rough against the uproar. In the dark, with all the firing and uproar, the men were getting a little confused and rattled.

All night the firing went on while the Marine battalion stood resolutely behind its perimeter. Crouching in the center of the position, the frail war correspondent, Stephen Crane, was thinking of the story he would write: *It was a night of terror, a thousand rifles rattling . . . the diabolic Colt automatic clacking, and the Mauser bullets sneering always in the air a few inches over one's head.* . . .

Beside Snavely, Private Jester lifted himself up to fire. Before he could pull the trigger, a bullet caught him in the mouth. He gurgled and fell back, kicking at the ground with his heels. Snavely blasted at the impenetrable brush, screaming curses.

"Cut it out," somebody said, with the force of an order. "You can't see them, and you only give away our position."

It was the first time the Marines had experienced guerrilla warfare, as fought in the tropics. There was nothing to see, only the hissing bullets which came singing out at you from the trees and jungle. Then the enemy melted away in the night, only to return again.

With light, the firing slackened. Snavely was surprised to find only three men had been killed, and another half dozen wounded. The Spaniards couldn't hit the side of a barn with a rifle, he decided.

During daylight nothing much happened. Now and then a rifle bullet whined overhead. The patrols probed forward six or seven miles, all the way to a place called Cuzco Well. There they saw a blockhouse defending the well, and a large number of Spanish soldiers. But they were not attacked, and they made it back to report to Colonel Huntington.

"A well, eh?" Huntington said. "That's interestin'. Probably the only water supply for miles around."

The Marines were being supplied by sea, but if they could not clear and secure the area surrounding Guantanamo Bay, their mission would end in failure. Admiral Sampson's ships could not use the harbor while Spanish guns commanded the heights around it.

Night came, and this night was a repetition of the first. The Marines lost sleep and men, including the battalion sergeant major.

Shortly after full daylight had come Colonel Huntington sent strong patrols out again. And once more the Spaniards seemed to have melted away in the brush. "What the hell do they do — *siesta* all day?" Snavely complained. Unused to this form of warfare, the Marine officers kept their own men busy during the day, and the strain was beginning to tell.

But the patrols reported they had found no source of fresh water except near the Spanish blockhouse at Cuzco Well.

"That settles it," Huntington said to his officers. "I've had a bellyful of this defending on a hill. Captain Elliott, you take Company C and Company D and march to Cuzco Well. Perhaps if their water supply is destroyed, the Spanish will withdraw."

Early the next morning C and D set off, filing out of the battalion perimeter and marching to the southeast. The day was hot and the men were bathed in sweat before they had gone five hundred yards.

Snavely, in the van with Quick, rasped, "They can give this country back to the Spaniards for all I care."

In about two hours the companies reached the wells. The Spanish were horribly lax; there were no patrols out and the men on guard were dozing. Without doubt, they figured the stupid *Americanos* were swatting mosquitoes back on the hills surrounding Guantanamo Bay.

From the ridge over Cuzco Well, Captain Elliott could see the whole area well enough. He called to Lieutenant Magill, a platoon leader. Lying along the ridge five yards away, Snavely could hear the two officers conferring.

"I make about six companies down there — more than half of them look like Spanish regulars. About three-to-one odds. Mr. Magill, take your men around to the other side of the position. I want you to cut off any chance of their retreatin'."

Magill grinned through his sweat. "Aye, aye, sir."

Magill's platoon moved out. Behind him Snavely heard Mr. Crane scratching away with his pad and pencil. The correspondent had insisted on coming along, although it had been obvious the captain hadn't liked it much.

The bulk of C and D lay along a semi-circular ridge facing the Spanish blockhouse. From the ridge they could see Magill's men moving into position. Snavely mopped sweat from his forehead and tested the action of his rifle once again.

Captain Elliott stood up to his full length on the ridge and waved. Far out to sea, Snavely knew, glasses on the bridge of the *Dolphin* were trained inland. Elliott was plainly visible through a good glass to those waiting naval officers. The Marines were calling for fire support at last.

Elliott leaped back down the ridge, sank down beside Snavely. >From the ridge he had been visible to the Spanish, too, and several Mausers had opened up.

Kapow! Kapow!

Snavely had learned to hate that sound these past few nights. A Mauser made a different sound from an American rifle. It was higher-pitched, more ringing than the black powder Krags and Springfields. Its slugs passed not with a loud buzz but with a whiplike crack.

Alerted, the Spanish were falling in down below, their officers and *sargentes* squalling. It sure took a lot of hollering to get them ready to fight, Snavely thought. Their bayonets and machetes flashed in the sun, and the officers had drawn long straight infantry swords of bright Toledo steel.

Snavely took aim at a dirty white packet with tarnished braid on the shoulders and took up the slack on the trigger. At the same instant *Dolphin's* big naval rifles sent their shells screaming into the Spanish position. Fire and metal splashed the blockhouse and the Spanish ranks kneeling around it. Some of the rounds went too high, passing over the blockhouse and well and cracking into the ridge beyond.

"My God!" Captain Elliott shouted. "They are firing on Mr. Magill!"

He stood up and a wasp swarm of Mauser slugs whined about his head. He ducked down. It was certain death to stand again on the ridge.

"We've got to signal somehow."

Behind Snavely and Elliott, Mr. Stephen Crane cried out. "Look over there, Captain — a man — with a cloth on a stick."

"By God, it's Quick!" Snavely said. "It's Sergeant Quick, sir!"

Quick had fixed a piece of torn shirt to some sort of stick, and he was standing in full view of the enemy, semaphoring desperately toward the open sea. He was signaling the *Dolphin* to cease fire.

Kapow! Kapow! To Snavely, it seemed the whole damn Spanish Army had Quick in their sights. Suddenly one of the *Dolphin's* shells blew dirt and smoke into the air just below the silhouetted sergeant. A large cactus just behind him flew apart under the impact of bullets and fragments.

Stephen Crane, huddling under the bullet swarm, was writing in his pad: *As he swung his clumsy flag to and fro, an end of it once caught on a cactus pillar, and he looked over his shoulder to see what had it. He gave the flag an impatient jerk. He looked annoyed.*

Suddenly the *Dolphin's* fire ceased. Quick's message had gotten through.

"A very brave man, Captain," Mr. Crane was saying.

But Captain Elliott was shouting, "Let's go! Let's go! Charge!"

With a howl of fury the Marines went down the ridge, their long rifles rattling.

Let's see how you like it now, chili bellies, Willis Snavely thought grimly. *Shoot at a man from behind bushes, in the dark, will you —*

Running forward, Snavely could see Spaniards falling right and left. The deadly accurate Marine fire, even on the run, was taking a ghastly toll of the white ranks. And from their rear, Magill's boys were pouring it on, too.

A Spanish officer was running forward. *"Adelante! Adelante!"* A Marine bullet took him in the stomach, bowled him over. Snavely went forward over his writhing form, seeing with half an eye. A .45-70 slug tore a hell of a hole in a man.

Afterward, Willis Snavely would admit that a lot of the Spaniards had courage. But they were outclassed. Huntington's Battalion were no ninety-day militia — they were Regular Marines who had been given rifles and knew how to use them.

Snavely brushed aside a Spanish saw-edged bayonet, thrust his own point home and heard his victim's death scream. He pulled the long steel free, looked around for more, then saw that the Spanish ranks were breaking.

The Cuban loyalists ran first while their Spanish officers shrieked imprecations at them. Then, with half their force melting away, the Spanish troops were running, too.

From his hill Mr. Magill's men blazed away at the fleeing companies, but there were too many Spaniards for him to stop them all. Many of them got away.

The firing died away as Elliott's two companies closed in on the blockhouse. A Spanish officer came out with a dirty linen flag tied to his long sword.

"Cease fire!" the captain ordered sharply.

Behind the enemy officer about two dozen privates were throwing down their arms. The officer took his sword and handed it to Elliott.

"Por Dios, señor —" There were tears in his eyes.

The Marines took the sword and the machetes from the belts of the captured Spaniards. Those pigstickers made them nervous. A quick count showed there were more than two hundred dead and wounded Spaniards on the ground.

Snavely, looking around, could see that almost none of their own boys had caught it. Mr. Magill was reporting to Cautain Elliott who was testing the long Spanish sword against the ground. It seemed he could bend it almost double without breaking the blade.

"All right," the captain said. "Smartly now. Let's blow up this damn well."

They destroyed the well and they marched back to camp. There, Elliott and Magill reported their success to Huntington who said he would recommend Sergeant Quick for the Congressional Medal. Mr. Crane said that all America would hear of the battle for Cuzco Well.

Maybe they did and maybe they didn't, Snavely figured later. He didn't care much what civilians thought, as long as they quit mistaking Marine dress blues for the Salvation Army uniform. If these damn correspondents could do something about that, they were worth the trouble they made.

Somebody told him that the Spanish fleeing from Cuzco Well had reported being attacked by 10,000 Americans. Perhaps Havana believed them, for with the well dynamited, all Spanish forces near Guantanamo withdrew. The base was secure.

The men of the battalion, from Lieutenant Colonel Huntington down to Private Willis Snavely, experienced a deep, quiet pride the day they came back to the United States, and the bands played *There'll be a Hot Time in the Old Town Tonight* as they paraded down Pennsylvania Avenue in front of the White House. They had landed on a hostile shore, captured an advanced naval base and held it. Nobody had ever done that before.

They got a hero's welcome and some ladies' organization presented each man in the battalion with a Bible. They even were treated to a few drinks. But better than that, Willis Snavely found, the girls by this time learned the difference between a Salvation Army officer and a United States Marine.

The United States Navy found Guantanamo Bay an ideal harbor. The Navy is still there and as a result of this action, the advance base concept took hold in naval circles. In 1902 the Corps organized an "advanced base" regiment, and in 1910 the Advanced Base School was established at New London, Connecticut, to be devoted purely to the study of amphibious warfare. Thirty years later the result of this experimentation was to become the decisive factor in a great Pacific war.

The Corps had found a mission.

With the end of the Spanish-American War, the United States was a world power with possessions around the globe. These possessions, and their neighbors, misruled for centuries, were in a state of virtual anarchy. Flushed with victory, pugnacious, and yet with a genuine feeling that it was setting the world to rights, the United States embarked on what was called the "large policy" in Latin America.

Our neighbors to the south — poor, illiterate, diseased and dictator-ridden — were to be cleaned up whether they liked it or not. The Marines who had found a new mission had also now to learn a new trade.

For under the "large policy" the bulk of the Marine Corps spent the first thirty years of the Twentieth Century in the Caribbean, stamping out one political hot spot after another. Between 1906 and 1917 Marines intervened in Cuba eight separate times. President Wilson inaugurated a policy of intervening in any nation where a new government had come to power by other than constitutional means. Order was always restored, but it meant work for the Marines.

The choice in the Caribbean has never been between freedom and tyranny, as many believe. It is between order and anarchy. Until they were withdrawn in the 1930's the Marines kept order.

Three

Instrument of Policy: Haiti 1915-19

The three most efficient military-constabulary organizations in the world are the United States Marine Corps, the French Foreign Legion and the Canadian Northwest Mounted Police. Each in its own field is supreme.
Theodore Roosevelt, President of the United States.

Just after dusk of a steamy July evening, while the snake skin drums thumped wearily in the hills, four oddly-assorted men were meeting quietly and secretly in a house in the little town of Grande Rivière, a dozen miles inland from Cap Haitien. The town itself was dark and silent; with the coming of night men barred their doors against the evil which walked by night.

The entire northern department of Haiti was aflame with the Caco War, a prolonged guerrilla conflict that had tied down two thousand, five hundred men of the Haitian Gendarmerie and the thousand-man brigade of Marines which had been sent to help them. Spies of the Cacos were everywhere, and for this reason the four men came furtively to the meeting house, hidden by the surrounding Haitian night.

Inside, with the blinds drawn, the pale candle light gleamed on four very different sweating faces. Standing back from the table was Jean Edmond Francois, a strapping Haitian Negro in the uniform of the Gendarmerie. Francois, trained in the American-run Garde d'Haiti, could read and write, a great accomplishment in these remote foothills. His broad face was intelligent and alert as he watched the other three men grouped about the crude table.

Leaning forward was the man called Conzé a slender, brown-skinned citizen of some standing in Grande Rivière. He seemed nervous in the close, stifling heat. He was a man embarking on a very dangerous game and he knew the slightest slip after this night would mean a horrible death.

The other two men wore the same uniform as Jean Edmond Francois, but with the bars of officers on their shoulder straps. The smaller man, William Button, sat calmly, listening intently. He would have the least part in the great drama that was unfolding here in Haiti, but it was a very important part, one that must not fail. He wore the single bar of a lieutenant, but he thought of himself as a corporal in the United States Marine Corps.

The fourth man held the attention of all. Six feet tall, with light blond hair and brawny forearms, he showed the lean, high-cheek-boned face of an Indian in the flickering light. His eyes were deep-set and very pale, the cold eyes almost of a beast of prey He was a quiet, austere man who made few friends, yet he was a man who inspired absolute loyalty among those who worked with him. When he moved, the candle light shone from the silver bars of a Captain of Gendarmes resting lightly on his muscular shoulders.

His name was Hanneken, and he was a master sergeant in the United States Marines.

These men knew what they had to do. They remembered the day in August, 1915 when a howling mob had pulled President Guillaume Sam from his sanctuary in the French Legation and shredded him in the streets, drinking his blood. Guillaume Sam, President of Haiti, had been a particularly unappetizing chief of state, and no one wasted sympathy on him. But when presidents are torn to bits by mobs and legations violated, order has disappeared, and for some years now the United States of America had been pledged to keep order in the, Caribbean.

For if the United States did not, somebody else damned well would. The French, and the British, too, had made that clear, Monroe Doctrine or no. The day the United States failed to act in its own backyard, Washington knew, was the day some foreign power would seize a foothold there.

So Marines had landed, and with them had come Sergeant Herman Henry Hanneken. When the immediate trouble had been put down, one of the steps designed to bring permanent order to the fevered Negro republic was the reorganization of the native gendarmerie.

By treaty with the United States, the constabulary force was to be officered and administrated by the Marine Corps. Officers and NCOs on detached service were commissioned in the Garde d'Haiti; their job was to build a permanent force capable of keeping order.

In Haiti a gendarmerie officer was more than a policeman. He had to be a director of civil affairs, and in a disorganized country like Haiti, the very welfare of the common people depended on his judgment. It was a painful, frustrating job among a savage, childish people, and the old tropical perils of boredom, rum, and native women were always present in the remote rural districts.

By the fact that Sergeant Herman Henry Hanneken, of St. Louis, Missouri, had been commissioned a captain of gendarmes and given his own district something of his quality can be told.

But keeping order in the frightful anarchy that had gripped Haiti was no simple task. Haiti, in common with all the islands of the Caribbean, was a poor, disease-ridden, overpopulated land. Independence from France had brought it no freedom, just as independence had solved none of the problems of Cuba or Santo Domingo; all the islands were gripped in an economic bondage rooted in their basic agricultural economy.

But this was not Hanneken's problem, nor that of the United States Marines. The first and basic problem was to bring some semblance of peace and order to the island by stopping the wholesale robbery and murder that continually plagued it. The immediate task was to get rid of the Caco.

The Caco exists in all lands similar to Haiti. He is basically an outlaw, and the one thing that could be said for him is that he has very little opportunity to improve his lot through legal means. The Caco is sometimes regarded as a Robin Hood or a dangerous revolutionist, depending on the point of view. In Haiti, as elsewhere, certain politicians liked to describe the Caco as a gallant fighter because he stood against government in general and foreigners in particular.

But to the bulk of the peasantry the Caco is no hero. To the small subsistence farmers — who sometimes did not raise enough to eat — the Caco was a man who robbed and murdered, who took what he wanted from whoever was too helpless to stop him. The Caco normally expressed his extreme dislike for the situation the world was in by plundering whoever was handy and killing him if he protested.

The Caco is a born guerrilla. Conventions, even if he heard of them, do not bother him. He does not fight unless he has a ten-to-one edge, and he likes better odds to attack. When pursued and hard pressed, he melts aways, dissolving his roving bands, and the policing authority soon finds only a peaceful agriculturist who had hidden his rifle and machete away against the day the police leave for the next valley.

Often the people seem to be on his side — for the government cannot protect them, and they dare not make the Caco any angrier than he is.

Haiti was made for Caco warfare. The land is extremely hilly, covered by dense woods and broken by numerous valleys and rivers. Each fertile valley is a different world from the next. There are few roads and no communications. For a modern military force, believing in such newfangled notions as communications, supply lines and open battle openly arrived at, such country is hell itself.

The Caco can be controlled, but never by a civilized nation employing civilized means.

And in Haiti, as the Americans began to organize the gendarmerie, the Cacos found a leader. The Americans in a way, gave him to them.

Charlemagne Peràlte, one quarter white, was a member of the ruling mulatto aristocracy of Haiti. His family, powerful landholders in central Haiti, had sent him to France for legal training. On his return, Charlemagne went into government, but found poor success. Charlemagne Peràlte was seemingly unable to pick the winning side.

In 1916 he was found guilty of certain anti-American demonstrations, but due to the civilizing influence of the Marines, he was not executed. He was humanely sentenced to manual labor on the road gangs in lieu of death, which to a Haitian aristocrat was not only a fate worse than death; it was an insult. Peràlte was a man gifted with a flair for flamboyant oratory. He talked his guard — the only incident of desertion in the entire Garde history — into letting him go free, then convinced both the guard and his fellow prisoners to join him in the hills.

Charlemagne fell in with the Cacos and found his special niche. Very shortly, moving from Caco stronghold to stronghold, he had collected a large following. Under Charlemagne's burning oratory against order, against the government in Port au Prince and against the gendarmerie, all northern Haiti was quickly aflame. He became an immediate and painful thorn in the side of Colonel Wise, the Marine who served as general and commander-in-chief of the gendarmerie. Any one of the hundreds of companies of gendarmes and Marines under Wise's command could have wiped out Charlemagne's force in pitched battle — but they could not catch him.

Big forces he avoided. Small, noncom patrols he ambushed when he could. The *blancs* who fell into his hands would have been far better off had they died fighting.

As with many primitive peoples, Charlemagne's people had gruesome means of dispatching captives. They tied them to stakes and cut their ears and noses off. They used the big-bladed brush knives to slit open tender bellies, letting the pink intestines billow out before the bound men's eyes. If the operation was done with skill, the victims took a long time dying.

In the tropics many hardwoods grow. The wood from these trees makes superior charcoal which gives off great heat for considerable periods. The Cacos considered these coals excellent stuffers for opened stomachs as well as for application to certain other tender portions of *blanc anatomy*.

After a few gendarmes had died screaming at Charlemagne's stakes, any possible love between the Caco, and the Marine Corps died an equally violent death.

Finally, Colonel Wise stated publicly that the only way to end the Caco War was to nab Charlemagne. This made excellent sense to the staff, and an order was promptly issued: *Get Charlemagne.*

Major Meade, in charge of the northern districts, saw clearly that his Marine patrols, clumsy in the jungle, were never going to catch the Caco leader. But he thought he knew the man who could.

Colonel Wise's directive was passed on to Captain Hanneken who then was in charge of a detachment of gendarmes in the town of Grande Rivière.

Now in the close, shuttered room Hanneken talked softly to his little group. He talked in Creole, the guttural patois of the Haitian back country. Hanneken had an ear for languages. Many Americans knew French, the tongue of the Haitian upper class, but Hanneken had learned the peasant speech, thick and heavy with African root words.

He told them that Charlemagne's Intelligence was excellent. No American officer, no gendarme unit could move without his knowing.

It simply wasn't possible for anyone to go back into the hills and capture Charlemagne. Everybody agreed to this.

Then he talked a bit about the reward of two thousand dollars gold on the Caco's head, for which Marines, of course, were not eligible. The group noted that Monsieur Conzé attended closely. Hanneken knew his Haitians, and he had an idea.

Then Hanneken told them his plan. Sweating, they listened. Then, under the prodding of those pale eyes, they agreed. It was decided. And as the plan unfolded in the following days it proved once again that truth is often more bizarre than any fiction.

Several days later Conzé visited the house of the gendarme captain, openly. It is not known what they talked about, but the next morning a rumor swept the market place in Grande Rivière that the *blanc* had offended the man of substance, Conzé. Unable to bear the insult, the most excellent Conzé had fled to the hills, swearing to become a Caco. Not only that, Conzé had stolen the pearl-handled revolver of Captain Hannekin, a well known and much admired weapon. Conzé had made an excellent start, the gossips agreed.

And in the gendarmerie itself, it was a bad morning. It was discovered that Gendarme Jean Edmond Francois had deserted, taking all his arms and equipment. There was laughter in the market place.

The most excellent Conzé proved a great success as a Caco. It became known that he had stores of arms, never-failing supplies of food, and rum in prodigious quantities for true patriots. He had no trouble at all recruiting a sizeable force. By August he was the talk of Grande Rivière. He had put fire to a village, and his brave warriors stopped the women coming into town to trade, stripping them and robbing them.

Best of all, he sent letters into Grande Rivière, attacking Captain Hanneken as a coward, making graphic remarks concerning the captain's ancestry and personal habits. Truly, the drums began to say, Conzé was a great man.

The citizens of Grande Rivière, while enjoying the captain's discomfiture, were nervous. They came to Hanneken and asked him, politely, why the hell didn't he do something about Conzé.

Hanneken went into furious action. He rushed his patrols and units from one end of his territory to the other, but somehow they always missed Conzé.

Meantime, the estimable Conzé was now in communication with the great Charlemagne himself who was most interested in the humiliations wreaked on the gendarmerie. The letters were written by Charlemagne's private secretary, a former slave of the foreigners who had seen the light and deserted. His name was Jean Edmond Francois, and he was proving most useful to Charlemagne Peràlte, who was surrounded by a pack of illiterate boors unable to read or write.

At the end of August, Conzé boasted he had built a fort, which he named Capois, up in the hills east of Grande Rivière, half a day's march away. *Let Hanneken come take Fort Capois, if he dared — and if he didn't, soon Conzé would come for Hanneken.*

The regular Marines who were stationed nearby sent word to Hanneken that if his men suffered from broken legs or chills in the foot area, they would be glad to clean up Capois for him. So finally, Hanneken issued elaborate orders for a secret night attack on Conzé's stronghold.

Hanneken's gendarmes marched to Capois by night, and here an amazing thing happened — Conzé, instead of melting into the brush, stood and fought. There was a great amount of shooting and yelling, and all kinds of confusion.

Hanneken himself, pistol in hand, led the attack. His bugler, at his shoulder, saw Hanneken flinch and fall behind a bush as the bullets zipped near. A moment later Hanneken stumbled out of the bushes, a first aid bandage pressed against a red-streaked arm.

"Sound the retreat!" Hanneken shouted.

The bugler's jaw fell.

"Sound the retreat — double time!" Hanneken squalled.

Almost crying, the bugler put his horn to his lips and blew the call. Since the American officers had come, the gendarmerie had never once retreated. The bugler felt unclean, disgraced.

Captain Hanneken, holding his left arm and moaning, led the rush to the rear.

The news roared across northern Haiti like a shock wave. The Cacos had defeated the gendarmes in open battle! The terrible American captain, whom all feared, had escaped with his life only by running away!

In the market place, when gendarmes passed, the women spat. Hanneken, brooding in his house with his arm in a sling, heard some violent words from his brother Marines. In the hills Charlemagne

Peràlte sent Conzé his congratulations, enclosing a commission as a major general for the successful chief.

He suggested, and the studious Jean Edmond Francois wrote neatly, that it was time for Conzé to capture the town of Grande Rivière. Conzé replied that he needed more men than he had at present — but if the great Charlemagne would join him in person, the town could be taken easily. More, the *blancs* would be driven into the sea as in the old days.

Word got around of the impending Caco raid and in Grande Rivière a number of property owners sold out and moved to the Cape where the Regular Marines stood guard. Soon it was whispered with rolling eyes that Charlemagne himself had come out of the hills with thousands of his men, and was now at Fort Capois. Grande Rivière's days were numbered, for the Garde captain still sat in his house, doing nothing.

One night a slight, brown form slipped unseen into the captain's house. What word was passed, no one knows, but on the last day of the month Captain Hanneken assembled ten of his best men, with Lieutenant Button. They noticed that his bad left arm had made a miraculous recovery; there was no puckered bullet hole, only a few streaks, as of red ink.

"Strip off your uniforms," he told them. He threw the gendarmes a pile of dirty rags to wear, similar to those the Cacos sported.

The gendarmes were disgraced. Only the terrible pale eyes of the captain and the discipline the Marines had bred into them kept them from rebelling. Were they going to sneak away, disguised?

Then Hanneken took out a stain which legend says he obtained from a voodoo priestess, and covered his own naked hide and that of Button's a rich brown. Then they left the house and slipped out of Grande Rivière, passing the gendarme patrols easily.

They crossed the river to a place called Mazaire. Here any attackers of Grande Rivière must pass. Within minutes they counted more than seven hundred Cacos passing within yards of their hiding place.

William Button knew the score, but the ten gendarmes did not. They only knew they were surrounded by hundreds of the enemy, and if they were discovered, they would go to the torture stake with the whites. They fingered their good Springfield rifles and their eyes rolled white.

Then three shots racketed from across the river. It was Conzé's signal for the massive attack on Grande Rivière. Over there firing broke out and the Lewis gun of the defenders chattered. In the bushes Hanneken and Button sweated, listening to the attack develop.

"Hsst!" A rifle bolt slid home, but the dark form slipping out of the night was already at Hanneken's side.

"Quiet!" Hanneken hissed to the crouching gendarmes.

Then he gripped the hand of Jean Edmond Francois.

Panting from fear and exertion, Jean Edmond told him that the great Charlemagne was a truly modern commander. Instead of leading the attack, he was going to direct operations from Fort Capois, waiting until the dust settled.

Hanneken, who had expected Charlemagne to pass Mazaire, could have cursed. But he was not that kind of man; legend has it that he said nothing. Across the river the firing had all the sounds of a serious battle being pushed home. The men led by the excellent Conzé were perfectly sincere about what they were doing, and what they were doing was reducing Grande Rivière stick by stick.

For months Sergeant Herman Henry Hanneken had planned and plotted, and now, just when Charlemagne seemed ready to pop into his hand, everything had gone to hell in a hand basket. Matters were now beyond control.

In luring Charlemagne down from the hills to Grande Rivière, Hanneken knew he had been playing with fire. Now he was about to get burnt — and a hell of a lot of other people with him over in the besieged town.

He said to Jean Edmond Francois, "Take us to the place where Charlemagne is camped."

When the deserter nodded, he turned and briefed Button as to what they were going to do. Button paled but nodded. Then he jerked his head toward the ten gendarmes. *"Allons!"*

In Hanneken's belt were two pistols, and Button held a Browning automatic rifle. Each of the gendarmes carried a service Springfield. It was light armament against a Caco army.

The night was hot and dark, partly overcast. Moving as fast as men could walk, Hanneken's group panted toward Fort Capois. Finally, exhausted, they completed the half-day's march by midnight.

Jean Edmond revealed that Charlemagn's camp was up on the crest of a wooded, rocky hill, rising just before them. There were many outposts — Charlemagne believed in good security.

Suddenly they were challenged in guttural Creole. But Jean Edmond knew the password. "*General Jean,*" he hissed, the word that had been set in honor of Jean Conzé.

As the Caco, outpost crowded around in the dark, Jean Edmond told them that his party brought great news to the leader — Grande Rivière had fallen.

With loud shrieks of jubilation at the prospect of much loot, the outpost let them pass through.

"There are five more outposts on this trail," Jean Edmond warned Hanneken. "It is more prudent that we leave the trail and try to slip past them."

"Nix," Hanneke'n said. "I ain't going to miss out on Charlemagne because I got lost in the dark. Move out!"

One by one they encountered and passed through four more outposts. The nerves of all of the gendarmes were screaming, and Button was bathed in sweat. But Hanneken showed no emotion, only an impatience to get up the hill.

The last standing patrol was Charlemagne Peràlte's personal bodyguard. Just beyond it a dying fire sent a red glow across a rocky clearing; dark forms moved about beside the fire.

"He is there, *mon capitaine,*" Jean Edmond whispered, trembling slightly. "By the fire — " Suddenly, the deserter was gone, slipping off in the dark.

A huge Negro who matched Hanneken's six feet stepped up to the Marine with pistol cocked. Hanneken muttered the password. The big Caco hesitated — perhaps he detected something false in the accent. But Hanneken refused to stay and talk; he brushed past the guard arrogantly.

Behind Hanneken came Corporal William Button, but the Caco saw the BAR. "Wait," he yelled. "Where did you get such a pretty gun?"

Button, who lacked Hanneken's gift of tongues, pressed on behind Hanneken, pushing the greedy hands aside. In the sudden, flaring light of the fire Hanneken saw a man peering at him across the flames.

This man, a light brown in color, wore a silk shirt straight from Paris, and in his belt hung the pearl-handled pistol that Conzé had "stolen." The pistol clinched it for Hanneken; he drew and fired, his sight steady on the shimmering silk cloth.

Instantly Button leaped back, whirled his BAR to his hip and sprayed the camp.

A woman, screaming shrilly, threw a blanket over the fire, and the darkness closed in abruptly. There were only the vicious howls of the Cacos, the shrieks of women, and the orange slash of rifle flashes in the rocks. Hanneken hit the ground, pistol in hand. He crawled forward, seeking, until his hand touched a silk shirt. The man inside it was quite dead.

Just beyond the body was a little depression in the rocks. Hanneken pushed the limp body into this and tumbled after it. The firing was reaching insane proportions all about him now. Out in the dark were Button and his ten men, and it was better to just lie low.

Thus Hanneken passed the night, huddled with the silk-shirted corpse. Several times he fired his pistol at shapes which came too close. He was fired on, but remained untouched.

The Cacos could not know what had happened, and the camp was in a panic. With light breaking, men entered the clearing, crying that the attack on Grande Rivière had been repulsed. Charlemagne could not be found. The Caco army broke up and moved toward the safety of their distant hills.

As the sun came up, Button and his ten gendarmes came up to Hanneken's hole in the rocks. Following his example, they had drawn back to wait out the night; now the Cacos were in full retreat. Hanneken and Button counted nine dead Cacos near the ashes of the fire, victims of Button's burst with the BAR.

The man in the silk shirt looked very small and dirty, and he was beginning to smell. They found a horse on the slopes of the hill, and the corpse was draped over it. Then Hanneken's party moved back down the trail to Grande Rivière, fired on frequently by roving Cacos. From there the small brown body was sent on to Cap Haitien where the archbishop, who knew the family, identified it as Charlemagne Peràlte.

The remains of the *chef de révolution*, were displayed publicly in each city of Haiti so no voodoo might develop. The body was buried under Marine Headquarters.

The gendarmerie wanted to shoot Jean Edmond Francois out of hand until Captain Hanneken did some tall explaining. In time Jean Edmond and the estimable Conzé divided the golden reward on Charlemagne's head.

With Charlemagne's death the Caco movement sputtered. Within a year the last Caco leader laid down his arms. Order returned to Haiti.

For his actions in bringing down Charlemagne, Sergeant Herman Henry Hanneken, with Corporal William Button, was awarded the Congressional Medal of Honor, a great honor and satisfaction to any man.

Ephemeral, those days in 1918. As jaunty as the tilt of a steel helmet with the globe and anchor device, but as brief as the flare of a lucifer — or the life of a rifleman in the Bois de Belleau.

Yet in a few brief weeks many thousands of men can die, and a Corps can cover itself with a glory never before known.

There is a bitterness over those days, too, for it was never possible to make the world safe for democracy; many historians regard the Great War as one which never should have been fought. This the regulars of the 4th Marine Brigade hardly knew or cared. The country needed them and they were there.

In 1917 America, belligerent as always and, as always, completely unprepared, found herself at war with the Central Powers. She had almost no guns, not even enough rifles. Worse, she had few trained men.

The National Guard held high promise, and Selective Service would bring in manpower, in time. But there was no time. America's Allies were bleeding to death, and forces in being were essential now, not some time in the future.

Because of its "large policy" in the Caribbean, the USMC had grown to 13,000. To it came a familiar order: *Detached by order of the President for service with the United States Army.* Much as Huntington's Battalion had been formed, a Brigade of 9,400 men was formed and attached to the 2nd Division (Regular) of the US Army.

General Pershing, A.E.F. Commander, said, "I wish I had a half million Marines."

As it turned out, he didn't need quite that many.

Four

Forces in Being: Belleau Wood 1918

"These were the old breed of American regular, regarding the service as home and war as an occupation. Rifles were high and holy things to them."
Colonel John W. Thomason, Jr., Marine artist-writer.

Across the ancient fields of Picardy a fourteen-mile long caravan of French *camions*, driven by tiny, imperturbable Annamese, roared easward toward the valley of the Marne. The old vehicles chugged through the environs of Paris, past the smoking arms factories; they went across the Ile de France and headed north, toward the sound of the guns.

In the back of a *camion*, talking slang, singing from time to time with his buddies of the 6th Marines, sat Cameron Albright, late of Illinois by way of Parris Island, South Carolina. He was a tall, rangy, young man, not quite twenty, with clear gray eyes under his short blond hair. On his head, tilted forward, was a wide campaign hat, sacred not to the skies of old Europe but to the brassy sun of the land from which he came. Between his knees, as between the legs of the shorter, dark Sim Kelly on his left and the voluble Yale man, Peabody, on his right, rested an oiled and gleaming Springfield rifle.

Cam Albright was thinking about that song — *How you gonna keep 'em down on the farm, after they've seen Paree?* Well, he hadn't seen Paree yet, but he sure as hell wasn't going back to the farm.

He was a United States Marine.

Cam didn't know where the *camions* were going — hell, even the officers didn't know, only the Frenchies who were guiding the busses — but he had a pretty good idea of what was going on. With Josh Peabody along, a man couldn't help but be informed. Peabody didn't make a big thing over having been to college, but he just couldn't close his yap. More, he bought the Paris newspapers each morning and translated the war news.

Ludendorff and the Imperial German Army stood above Paris this May of 1918, the apparent dictators of Europe. Along the Somme, the British Fifth Army had been shattered, and the demoralized French Sixth Army was pulling back from the Aisne. The war was damned close to being lost, and at last somebody had given the order to the American Expeditionary Force: *Go north and fight*.

They had been training for a long time. Of course, the British and French had been at it for almost four years, and they thought they knew all the answers. Their instructors had tried to pass it on to the new American divisions.

First the Limeys and their bayonets — the bayonet will win the war. Cut and thrust, lunge and parry, butt stroke and smash, till your arms shook and you couldn't hold your piece steady.

Then the Frogs with their hand grenades — the hand grenade will win the war! Pull the pin, throw, hit the dirt, watch the pieces fly. Do it again, till you wished you'd never seen one of the damn things!

But Private Kelly had summed it up for the whole platoon, when he'd said, "If they think I'm going to chase some Heinie until I'm close enough to hit him with a grenade or stick him, they're nuts!"

Cam agreed, gripping his rifle tighter in his hard young hands. *Here's your wife, Marine!* That's what they'd told him, when the shining blue steel was pressed into those hands, to have and to hold, to respect and to cherish, so long as he stayed in the Corps.

It was a marriage almost a year old for Cam Albright. Soon it would be consummated — in blood.

In Versailles, where even the polished brilliance of the mirrors could not dispel the gloom, the Sixth Session of the Supreme War Council was opening. The members could hear the growl of German guns as they convened; already the Krupp monster, Big Bertha, vomited shells on Paris. Château-Thierry had fallen, and now the Hun turned westward, toward the sacred capital of France. Already a million civilians had left Paris. The government had packed its files.

The Council knew that the supreme commander, Marshal Foch had guessed wrong as to where the Germans would strike, and that the May assault on the Aisne behind Chamin-des-Dames had turned into sheer disaster for the French: thirty miles lost in seventy-two hours, with sixty thousand prisoners, almost seven hundred field pieces, and two thousand machine guns swallowed up by the advancing Imperial German Army.

The Chamber of Deputies had met in secret session and had been told that the war might end in three weeks — disastrously. The Supreme War Council might never meet again.

At Versailles, Clemenceau, Premier of France, rose to speak. His opening statements dealt with his disappointment with the Americans, of whom the people of France had heard much but seen little. . . .

The American Expeditionary Force had seen little action in the Great War by May, 1918. Allied officers had not considered American troops ready for the line, since they knew nothing of trench warfare, and further, they urgently desired to use the fresh Americans as fillers for their own depleted units. Having no confidence in American military leadership, Marshal Foch insisted that small American units fight as part of existing Allied divisions, under Allied command.

But Black Jack Pershing was equally stubborn on this point — Americans had come to fight, but they would fight as a National Army, under their own officers. The controversy had dragged on, becoming involved in politics during the winter of 1917-1918. Finally, events threw the decision General Pershing's way.

With the British Fifth Army destroyed on the Somme and the French forces reeling backward from the Aisne, Ferdinand Foch recalled what he had been told by Pershing when the Americans had arrived: *We are here to fight and be killed. Do with us as you will, without counting.*

Pershing did not object to overall French command, so long as the tactical integrity of American forces was upheld. Now, the French had no more time to argue the matter. Swift orders went to the A.E.F.

On May 30th, German units held ten miles along the north bank of the Marne, and their patrols were across the river. There were no French forces between them and Paris capable of holding, and it was impossible to transfer troops from other parts of the front over the strained transportation system.

Only the uncommitted American Expeditionary Force was available, and now it rolled to the sound of the guns.

In the *camion*, Private Josh Peabody was rattling off the names of the French towns as the column bounced through. Montmirail, Pontoise, Gisors. "Napoleon fought his last battles before Elba here," he said. His thin-nosed face and dark eyes were excited, seeing the historic towns and villages. He was a college boy, one of the few who had diluted the regular ranks of the Corps since war had been declared. Most of them had become officers, but Peabody said he didn't want that.

"Look there, Cam — see that hotel? Hotel de La Tour d' Auvergne!" Peabody told them all the story of Napoleon's Grenadier, in whose honor it had been decreed that his name should never be removed from the roll of his company, and when that roll was called, a soldier of France should answer: *Dead. Dead, on the field of honor.*

Cam could understand that. The Marines had that kind of *esprit*, too, though they wouldn't be so flamboyant about it.

But now the Marine Brigade was passing through streams of fleeing French civilians, none of whom showed any of the spirit of La Tour d' Auvergne. The honking *camions* pushed them off the roads where they shook their fists at the Marines passing by.

This was a region of France which showed clearly the sufferings of four years of war, whose population was in the depths of despair. The people had heard of the Americans, but they had not seen them, and now, seeing them, they hardly cared. The terrible Hun Army was on the move, and they were running to the south, taking with them whatever pitiful possessions they could carry.

Cam saw a young woman wheeling a baby carriage, her thin face gray with exhaustion. An old woman, hobbling and groaning, herded along a pair of goats, the most valuable things she possessed in the world. The old and the sick lay alongside the road, crying for help to unheeding ears. The road was jammed with thousands of their kind, plus all the flotsam of a beaten army moving to the rear.

Small units and individuals of the French forces straggled by, officers and men, pushing the civilians out of their way, tired, bloody, uncaring, anxious only to leave this terrible war behind.

The French Army in many ways was the best in the world, but it had been asked to stand in the breach too often; through the stupidity of its command, it had been asked to die vainly one time too many. Now, many of its men had had enough.

All day the *camions* of the Second Division and the Marine Brigade pushed their way against the tide of fear.

Once, near dark, while the *camions* halted, a brigade of French cavalry passed the column — smart, erect, good horses with harness jangling. The faces of the horsemen were turned to the front.

Private Kelly said, "Boy, the Heinie machine guns'll fix their clocks — "

Peabody was lifting a hand in a short salute as the French officers exchanged salutes with the officers of the Marines.

Cam Albright thought of something Peabody had said. *Dead, dead on the field of honor.* Cam Albright, farm boy from Illinois, was thinking that the spirit of French gallantry was not dead.

The cavalry brigade rode up the road and disappeared. In a few minutes the two regiments of the 4th Marine Brigade took to the road again.

In the north, the men riding the *camions* could hear a sullen rumbling. Cam wondered, suddenly, who would answer to the next roll of the 6th Marines.

James Harbord, Lieutenant Colonel of Cavalry on the regular list, but holding a commission of brigadier in the new National Army — "Mex" rank, the Army called it — had relieved Marine General Doyen as commander of the 4th Brigade in early May. Doyen, who was desperately ill, returned to the States, where he would not live to see the end of the war. Harbord, whom Doyen's heartbreak had given a chance for glory, had assumed command of the Marines with some trepidation.

How would these sea-going soldiers, largely veterans, react to an aging cavalryman, still untried in battle, leading them into combat?

But the Marine colonels, Catlin and Neville, who were actually senior to Harbord on the regular list, had taken the change in stride. There had been no troops in formation at the change-over, no field music, no flashing sabers and colors. There was only a quiet reading of orders, then handshakes all around. And Wendell Neville, holder of the Congressional Medal, had said something to James Harbord he would not soon forget:

"Sir, the motto of the Corps is *Semper Fidelis.* You can count on us."

Now, Harbord, a quiet, good-looking man with gray hair topping his square-chinned soldier's face, who had come ahead of the main

column with his small staff, thought, *It will be a miracle if my outfit reaches the front at all. If the Germans catch us on the move —*
It was proving no easy matter to move a division of 28,000 men. When it had received orders to proceed to the valley of the Marne, the 2nd Division had been billeted in twenty-eight separate villages, the 9,400 man Marine 4th Brigade alone spread over miles of countryside.

The staffs of the A.E.F. were untrained in motor movements; the Army had only gotten its first trucks in 1916, and the Marines were more used to ships than roads. The French had charge of both rails and highways, and sometimes communication was slightly less than zero. Fortunately, when the troop units had gotten out of the busses, French officers rode the *Camions,* and Harbord hoped they knew where they were going.

He was brigadier commanding, but they hadn't told him.

He was supposed to get final instructions on the march. The galleys and heavy equipment of the brigade were loaded on railroad cars, to catch up with the main column later.

Driving up the Metz-Paris highway toward the battlefront, Harbord had finally reached Mareuil in late evening of the last day of May. The swollen flow of refugees had made movement of a single staff car difficult. Word reached Harbord here that he was to outpost the west side of the Ourcq River.

While he was reconnoitering, a French staff officer approached him. *"Monsieur le général de la Brigade de Marine?"* It seemed his orders had been changed; now he was to defend the east side of the Ourcq.

With his Adjutant, Major Harry Lay, his interpreter, Martin Legasse, and his Army aide, Norris Williams II, late of Harvard, Harbord shoved off again. His administrative officer, Major Holland M. Smith and Marine aide, Fielding Robinson, were back on the road to guide the troops in.

Harbord scouted west of the Ourcq to a village called Bremoiselle. Here he found a suitable place for brigade headquarters. The village looked as if the Germans had already arrived; it had been looted and vandalized by retreating *poilus* of the French Army.

Here Harbord decided to leave Harry Lay and Legasse while he and Lieutenant Robinson went back to the highway looking for the incoming brigade.

Lay, a chunky Princetonian long in the Corps, smiled cynically under his short, brush moustache. "Hell, General, you don't obey orders from the French on just Change one or two — Change three is probably on the way now."

But Harbord went back to the road. He never saw Bremoiselle again.

On the highway near the town of Meaux he and Williams passed several retiring units of the French forces. Then they saw a staff car bearing the two stars of a *général de division*. At Harbord's signal and salute, the portly major general dismounted.

Norris Williams II, in addition to Harvard, had attended school in Switzerland. In nearly flawless French, he asked for Harbord: "I am very much in need of information before selecting a position for my brigade. Can you tell us how near are the French troops east of here? How far are the Germans? Where is your own command?"

Williams didn't have to translate the swift reply, *"Je ne sais pas, mon général."*

"May I ask where you are going, sir?"

"La soupe!" The general of division was going to dinner, and that was all he knew about the situation.

The quiet James Harbord said a few unprintable words on his way back to Meaux. He didn't know where most of his staff was; he didn't know where his brigade was or when it was coming; worst of all, he didn't even know for sure where it was supposed to make its stand.

And he had been told earlier he might expect to be under attack before morning!

Private Cam Albright awoke from a half-doze as the *camion* screeched to a halt; the only way the tiny brown Annamite driver knew to halt the lurching bus, it seemed, was to throw on the brakes while traveling at full speed. Growling, the Marines in the vans of the *camions* came awake.

"What's up?" Kelly asked angrily.

The French officer in charge of the convoy ran back along the side of the road, shouting.

"Allez! Allez!"

"I'd like to get you in the back alley myself," the small Sim Kelly snapped.

"He wants us to dismount," Peabody told him, yawning.

Cam owned no watch, but he guessed it was close to midnight. Not long before, the column had gone through a place called Meaux. Must be close to the front. He was aware of the sound of big guns north and west; with the other men beside him he suddenly came awake.

He lifted his cold rifle, adjusted his kit bag with the round, soup-bowl steel helmet on top, and swung down from the back of the *camion*.

"Where the hell are we?"

"Stow the talk — stow the talk! Fall in!" Monk Wallace, the squad leader was moving up and down, growling. Monk was past thirty, a big, slope-shouldered Westerner, a perennial private in the Corps who had finally made corporal when so many of the top NCOs had accepted commissions during the current expansion.

The busses were pulling off the road for miles, front and rear. Cam saw there were going to be Marines scattered up and down the highway from hell to breakfast. He was glad he didn't have the job of getting them organized.

A captain ran by, shouting something about Change 3 arriving — the 6th Marines were supposed to be to the west, along another road, but hadn't got the word in time. The rest of the brigade had turned off, leaving them way out ahead.

"There's always ten per cent don't get the word," Kelly muttered unhappily. With a roar of motors, the *camions* turned around and sped southward.

All the Marines could hear the constant muttering, as of thunder, to the north now. They cracked a few jokes about it, in the dark. They were cold and stiff, and they hadn't had a decent meal or night's sleep for forty-eight hours, but no one said anything about that.

Somewhere high above, hidden by the night, a solitary airplane engine whined mournfully. Cam wondered what the hell he was doing up there by himself.

"Hey, watch the glim!" Kelly shouted at Private Peabody, who had fired a cigarette. Peabody, startled, dropped the match.

The airplane engine roared strongly; there was the sudden shriek of air split by falling bombs.

Brram! Brram-Bram!

"Watch out!" Monk Wallace yelled. "Get off the road!"

Some Heinie pilot up there had good eyes. Fortunately, he missed.

The long lines of Marines buckled out from the highway, thrashing into wheat fields. There they hunkered down, talking in monosyllables, cold, hungry, miserable.

It was a long time before General Harbord got word to them. They were to get some rest, if possible, in the fields. With daylight the brigade was to move north, to meet the retreating French lines. The firing, continuous now, seemed very close.

For four hours they waited in the damp fields, while German aircraft cruised up and down the highway, now and then dropping a stray bomb. At four-thirty, with light breaking in the east, the Marines rousted out from the dew-covered lilies of the valley whitening in the woods, and fell in.

No one knew where the galleys were. There was no hot coffee, no breakfast. They had a few tins of "goldfish" — a smelly variety of canned salmon — and some corned beef, if anyone wanted to eat. Neither dish was wildly popular in the dawn, but like Cam, most of the men ate. Like Monk Wallace, who had been around, said: "You guys don't know when you're going to eat again."

Then they shoved off, heading north.

In the midst of rolling farmland, wheat fields and pasture lands alive with the red buds of poppies in June bloom and dotted with light stands of timber and farm houses, stood the shattered town of Lucy-le-Bocage, smoking from artillery pounding. Its old houses and parish church had crumbled to new rubble, but oddly, a thing much noted by the men who passed by there this June morning, the great figure of the Saviour on the Cross in the church yard remained untouched by flying steel.

Just east of Lucy-le-Bocage began an irregular area of brush land, less than a mile square. Once it had been a hunting preserve for the lords of the ancient Château of Belleau. It was covered by what foresters would call second-growth timber, and it had not been underbrushed. Under the scrub lurked a scattering of huge, irregular boulders.

It was poor ground, unpicturesque, insignificant in size, and it had to this moment no past.

On the Marine maps it was marked as the *bois de Belleau*, or Belleau Wood. Here, the storm would break.

Arriving on a line running westward from Château-Thierry through the old village of Lucy-le-Bocage and beyond, Brigadier

General James Harbord, National Army, received the orders of the French commander of the 6th Armée: "Hold this line at all hazards."

This order, Harbord passed on to his regiments — the 5th Marines under Wendell Neville, and the 6th under Julius Catlin — which lay across the low ridges, looking out across the poppy-dotted wheat fields. Behind them, McCloskey's 12th Field Artillery had registered and stood ready, thousands of rounds beside the guns.

Now, within minutes of the first order, came a second: The Marines were to dig a line of entrenchments several hundred yards to the rear, just in case.

Harbord looked at Harry Lay, saw the sour smile on that blocky officer's face. Change two was here.

"To hell with that," Harbord stated. "Tell the French I have given orders to die if necessary to hold the present line. We shall dig no trenches to fall back to. The Marines will hold where they stand!"

The interpreters had quite a time, chewing that over, but the staff of the 4th Marine Brigade stood a little stiffer.

Down on the line, Cam Albright, Kelly and Josh Peabody crouched low along the ridge, rifle slings tight on their arms. Above them stood Corporal Wallace, peering out over the wide, open terrain to the front. He put a critical eye on the squad, said, "Peabody, get your ass down."

"Can't, Corporal," Josh said. "That's a Peabody ass, and it has a conformation all its own."

Somebody laughed and Wallace grunted. He looked back over the fields. Except for his steel helmet and bayonetted rifle, he could have been a D. I. back at the Island, standing on rifle range.

Now the 4th Brigade was under fire, as the long range artillery began to range in.

Wheee — eeee — eee — bram! Bram — brram!

Fired from long range, the German guns sent their projectiles on a high trajectory, allowing the sound waves made by the shell's passage to arrive before the impact. Sometimes, a man had five seconds to hunker down and hug the earth.

"They say you never hear the one that kills you," Peabody whispered nervously to Cam.

Cam looked at him. "No way to prove it, is there?" he said.

Cam had never been shot at before, and he was glad the old hands were around. There were men here who had served in China, the

Philippines, Mexico, Haiti. They had heard the bullets scream before. Colonel Catlin, the regimental C.O., had a Congressional Medal, just like old Sergeant Major Quick, down there. They had been around, and they knew what to do. None of them looked nervous — hell, this was their business.

By God, Cameron Albright suddenly decided, this was his business, too. He was a United States Marine, the same as they were.

The field guns barked now, over there. The 77s shrieked in, giving only a second's warning — or none at all.

Crump-blam! Flame blossomed high, and dirt and rocks showered the prone Marines, a fragment nicking Cam's cheek. He hadn't heard that one come in at all! Two men in the next squad were hurt, moaning softly.

"Austrian 88 — high velocity," he heard someone — he thought it was young Lieutenant Cates — say.

Way out there, across half a mile of rolling fields, Cam saw something. Not men — he couldn't see individuals at that distance — but moving tiny figures, almost like ants. They were coming in a giant wave that grew and spread across the landscape.

The sergeants and officers were checking the windage. With field glasses, someone was estimating the range. More than three quarters of the brigade were qualified marksmen who held a sleek Springfield — one of the sweetest rifles ever made — the way they would hold a woman.

Squeeze her right, and she'd perform for you!

Cam settled down, letting his bones hold his weight, the way he'd been taught during many painful hours of firing. He put his eye behind the leaf sight.

He picked out one of the tiny, moving targets across the waving wheat field, and he waited for the officers to give the order, *commence firing.*

Hauptmann Friedrich Kransky-Müller was keeping his men at a steady pace. A veteran officer, he knew the horrendous cost in German dead this war had exacted, and now that the Allied lines had cracked, it was vital to maintain the pressure, keeping the lines moving back, until the Imperial Army stood in Paris.

The enemy must never get another chance to dig in his *verdammten* machine guns! Kransky-Müller hated machine guns. They had stalemated this war, brought the hot courage of German youth to naught.

What avail was it to charge forward, in tight, disciplined column, into the hell of No Man's Land, criss-crossed by thousands of those damned machine guns?

Almost as much as the guns themselves, Kransky-Müller hated the stupidity of the high commanders who had been trained back in the days when the horse and saber were still potent weapons. They didn't know how to fight the machine gun, either, except by sending waves of men against it.

For three years, the life of an infantry officer of the line had averaged not quite sixteen days. The only saving grace, *Gott sei dank*, was that the British and French generals had gone to the same schools as the Prussians — they knew no better tactics, either.

Some day, Kransky-Müller thought with his engineer's brain, the fools will realize the only answer to a change in technology is more technology. The airplane and the tank, now — he could see *their* possibilities.

Fortunately, the General staff had realized before the Allies that the war must be made mobile again. No one would win it in the trenches. Since last year German troops had been training for the assault — massive barrages, then thin waves of infantry going forward — infiltrating, it was called — snapping around the enemy positions like the jaws of a steel trap.

Herr Gott, how it had worked against the British, this spring! They stood in place, like the indomitable bulldogs they were, while the German lines broke around them, swallowing them up. The war was back in the open fields again, this summer of 1918, and neither British bayonets nor French hand grenades would stop the German tide!

Keep them running, and their machine guns wouldn't help much, either.

With a round, blue eye on his advancing men, Kransky-Müller saw that they were tired. Only the fact that they were winning kept them going like this. A year ago, now, they would have been singing as they pushed along:

Ich heisse Annemarie, ein jeder kennt mich schön —
Ich bin ja die Tochter, von ganzen Bataillon!

Now they didn't sing, and increasingly he noted, that when the word was passed to halt, many of them fell asleep. But for all that, they were tough and veteran; God help whoever got in their way.

Kransky-Müller did not wonder that he was traversing the same path his grandfather had known in 1871, or that his own two-year old son might march down someday, unless an end came to the fratricidal mania that gripped European civilization. Nor did he think about the Socialists in the Reichstag who were threatening open revolt against the war.

He did not know that Constantin Fehrenbach, President of the Reichstag, had told von Hertling that Germany must win a victory, or else. Nor that Hertling, as chancellor, had given Marshal Ludendorff his orders.

The Prussian service was never an easy one, and there was no time for such thinking. *Hauptmann* Kransky-Müller knew only that he had orders to keep up the advance.

Spang!

Rifle fire, pecking at them from the low ridges far to the front. Kransky-Müller smiled. The range was at least six hundred meters!

"They are panicky, those chaps," he said aloud to his lieutenant, Benno Kirst. "Their officers have the jitters, to allow men to fire so prematurely — "

"*Jawohl, Herr Hauptmann.* Rifle fire is not effective beyond two hundred meters," the short, dark Kirst snapped. Since the time of the great Frederick, German troops fired only at close ranges, and only at an aiming point designated by a company officer. They did not pick individual targets, because it was useless to try to train common soldiers in marksmanship — but they blanketed an area by fire, counting on the law of averages to hit something.

Spang! Spang!

A sergeant grunted and collapsed.

"*Teufel!*" Kransky-Müller said. "*Vorwärts!*"

Since the days of the great Frederick, also, German troops had often been more afraid of their own officers than the enemy. The column went forward.

Up ahead, still at incredible range, the ridges blazed fire. Under the incessant, wicked cracking of fine Marine rifles, held true, more men bit the dirt.

Thoroughly angry now, Kransky-Müller bellowed, "Deploy!"

Now the long, skirmish lines of infiltrators ran forward, wave behind wave. Let the damned rifle shooters stop them now! It would take many machine guns with interlocking fire — but minutes later Kransky-Müller saw his command destroyed, long before closing with the enemy. He had never seen anything like it — the enemy must be using machine guns, after all!

Kirst was dead, lying face downward in the trampled wheat. The advance faltered. Most of the NCOs had fallen.

Kransky-Müller felt a paralyzing blow against his right leg. He fell to his knees. There was no pain — not yet — but he shook his fist at the blazing ridges and screamed, *"Teufel-hünde! Damned devil-dogs!"*

Then, while Kransky-Müller rolled on the ground in agony, a senior officer snapped, "Halt the advance! Dig in!"

As with the tide reaching its furthest advance upon a beach, the German onslaught paused, wavered, went forward, then ebbed abruptly.

The German troops fell down and, with the resignation of long practice, began to dig entrenchments. When they had finished, they dozed.

No one yet realized it, but the tide of war had turned.

James Harbord knew it was one thing to stop the advance of troops in open fields — and quite another to attack against prepared enemy positions. But he had an order from General Degoutte's Sixth Army Headquarters: *Counter attack. Drive the Boche back.*

The 4th Brigade was to clear the Bois de Belleau which lay just in front of its ridges. Harbord believed the Germans had not yet heavily occupied the wood and he hoped for surprise.

But the Marine front-line companies had done little scouting. The few French maps they possessed were extremely poor, and they weren't too much worried about what the Germans had done. The Marines, too, had lessons to learn in this war.

The Imperial Army had been stopped, but it had not been broken.

Harbord knew, as he gave the attack order, that every man in the brigade realized what was at stake. America herself, as well as the Marine Brigade was on trial. Black Jack Pershing had claimed Americans could fight as well as their British and French Allies; it was up to the 4th Brigade to prove it.

On June 6th, at dawn, Marines attacked in the Bois de Belleau. It took twenty days of hell to clear the woods.

By late afternoon of June 6th, Cam Albright's company had fought its way into the village of Bouresches, on the east side of the wood. It had been a bad day. First, Major Berry's Battalion from the 5th Marines had attacked the west side of the Bois de Belleau. Berry led his boys out across an open wheat field in line formation.

A few of them reached the wood. There they clung desperately, unable to move. At last, they made contact with elements of Sibley's 3rd Battalion, 6th Marines along the southern portion of the brush. That phase of the attack had been a bloody failure. Major Berry was hit, badly.

The 6th Marines did a little better. They took Bour-esches, at the eastern fringes of the wood.

The Germans were in the village, dug in along the roads, behind trees and rocks. Fire slapped at the advancing 96th and 79th Companies as they pressed forward.

"*Battle sight, fire at will!*" shouted Captain Duncan, as they closed with the Germans. A minute later, he was dead.

But the C.O. never dies. Lieutenant Clifton Cates, with Robertson, took the company into Bouresches.

Cam Albright, with Peabody on his left, heard the ripping snarl of a heavy Spandau machine gun. Dirt flew in front of him; he and the squad hit the ground. The Springfields cracked back, but the German gunners were dug in behind rocks, flanked by barbed wire and sharpshooter pits.

Monk Wallace started to shout something. He collapsed into the earth, his face a bloody ruin. Under the slapping, blazing fire, the company melted into small fragments, dispersed, hugging the ground.

They were already spread from hell to breakfast, Cam thought, and the officers couldn't tell what was happening. He yelled at Peabody, "We've got to get that gun!"

He saw Peabody's white-faced nod. Behind Peabody, Sim Kelly crawled up, panting. "Shoot the bastards!"

The three of them opened fire, working the bolts of their Springfields methodically. But the German gunners stayed low. Behind Cam, another man cried out and thrashed about.

"Pin 'em down," Kelly said suddenly, his round, stubby face working. He started to crawl to the left.

Cam laid his rifle on the machine gun nest, emptied a magazine into the area. Beside him, Peabody was firing and cursing, pulling out a fresh clip to reload.

He saw Kelly move forward some twenty-five yards, then leap to his feet. The black grenade sailed slowly upward in a high arc, leaving his hand.

Brrrrt — brrrt — brrrt! The Spandau spat furiously.

Blam!

Black smoke spurted from the German position.

Cam leaped to his feet, filling his lungs for screaming. He burst forward, leaping over the strand of wire where Kelly had fallen, his chest shot away by a hail of machine gun slugs. Behind the overturned Spandau, three Germans moved feebly, their faces covered with blood. Cam shot one through the head; Peabody brought down another.

The third German, helmetless, his hair hanging over a bloody forehead, threw up his hands, screaming at them.

Cam went back, checked Kelly, feeling sickness in his throat at the savage work of the machine guns. One machine gun — two men lost. In the hours and days to come, they would regard that as a good trade.

For the Germans had three lines of entrenchments across the Bois de Belleau, each wired in and supported by machine guns at every turn. There was no way to cross the wood except to reduce each position, each line of trenches, piece by piece as they came to it.

That was the way they took Bouresches and moved on beyond it. It was here that Floyd Gibbons, the famous correspondent, who had badgered General Harbord into letting him accompany the attack, had his left eye shot out. Thinking him dead, the Paris censor, his friend, allowed his last dispatch to go through as a last gesture, even though it mentioned the Marines by name and stated the name of Château-Thierry, the nearest large town.

Years later, the Marines were still trying to live down the unsought publicity that resulted. The Army Third Division took Château-Thierry, and no Marine would claim otherwise. After all, the Bois de Belleau was glory enough.

By June 7th, the mile square wood had turned into a corner of hell. Late in the night the Germans counterattacked.

Peabody, lying in a rifle pit along the front positions, was the first to give the alarm.

"Gas! *Gas!*"

Artillery shells had slammed in, spraying the Marine area with horrid, viscous liquid. Fumes rose quickly, blinding eyes, rasping throats, blistering soft skin with angry red burns.

Peabody filled his lungs to shout the warning — and sucked in a great quantity of mustard vapor. He got his crumpled mask on too late. He thrashed about in agony, choking, his eyes streaming hot tears.

Cam Albright crawled close to him, seizing his shoulder. Voice muffled by the gas mask, Cam said, "Get back to the aid station.

"No," Peabody wheezed. "They're coming — "

No Marine, so far, had gone voluntarily for treatment. Seared by blister gas, they stayed on line; hands or feet shattered, they carried on until they dropped from shock or fainted from loss of blood.

The Germans attacked through the clouds of vapor, later, but mustard gas was as hard on the attackers as the defenders. Stifled by masks, men could not move freely; through clouded goggles, they could barely see to shoot. And the awful liquid dripped from trees and bushes, deadly to the touch, imparting a fatal burn before a man realized he was a casualty.

Fire fights rippled along the line, but the Marine positions held. The enemy did not reach Bouresches.

When the firing died away, Peabody lay choking in his mask. On an officer's order, he was carried to the rear, with others who had been unlucky or slow.

Cam knew what mustard gas did to a man when he breathed it. The lungs blistered, formed huge, watery sacs. The blisters broke and broke again, for nothing could stop the action of the chemical. Often a man drowned in agony in his own fluids. Even slight burns were months in healing.

Cam never saw Josh Peabody again.

Now Belleau Wood crawled with both Marines and Germans, yards from each other in the underbrush, crouching behind rocks, meeting each other at bayonet point in the hastily dug trenches. It was continual, dirty close-in fighting.

Brigadier General Harbord had given the order to clear the Bois de Belleau. Bloodied, exhausted, the Brigade carried the order out.

It was to be a trial of nerves between the victors of a hundred European fields and the newcomers from across the water. And

Gunnery Sergeant Dan Daly, leading a platoon, showed what the nerves of the Marines were made of.

Come on, you sons of bitches! Do you want to live forever?

The brigade went into a mile square acre of hell, and more than half of them did not walk out. A thousand of them died there.

Shot to pieces within a few days, Cam's battalion was ordered out; a new unit took its place. New men came to take the places of Kelly and Peabody and the others.

There was hot food at last and, best of all, hot coffee but there wasn't too much rest, for German artillery searched the area by day and night.

Then, after a little time, the battalion went back in. The outfit that had replaced them was no longer fit for the line.

As the battalion moved by night through Gob Gully — Gobert Ravine, on the maps — the Germans must have suspected something. A barrage crashed down, splashing the night with fire and steel.

Brram! Deafened, Cam saw a Marine fall a few yards in front of him. Cam started for him, felt the lash of fire along his side as flying metal struck home. It felt like boiling water had been poured on him and he knew he was bleeding.

Cam Albright fell down. As he lost consciousness, he would have liked to tell Peabody that sometimes you did hear the one that got you. Only it was too late then to do anything about it.

He was still in the hospital when Major Shearer, 5th Marines, sent a message from the north end of Bois de Belleau to Brigadier General Harbord: *This wood now exclusively U. S. Marine Corps.* Harbord sent the message on to A.E.F. Headquarters, exactly as written.

Fifty-five percent of the 4th Brigade was dead or wounded, but the German General von Conta was reporting: *The effect of our gunfire cannot seriously impede the advance of American infantry....*

Cam Albright almost died in the hospital. He didn't make it back for the big push at Soissons in July where the A.E.F. with the Marines in the van broke the back of the Imperial German Army. He missed St. Mihiel and the long agony of the Argonne, and he was still not able to walk when word came that the Germans had asked for an armistice.

A little later, Private First Class Cameron Albright got to see Paris, after all. He didn't mind the way the girls reacted to a Marine uniform, but he didn't go for the *boulevardiers* throwing their arms around him and trying to kiss him.

The people of Paris had read the order issued by General Degoutte:

> *By reason of the brilliant conduct of the 4th Brigade of the 2nd U.S. Division in taking the village of Bouresches and the important terrain of the BOIS DE BELLEAU, defended by a numerous enemy, the Commanding General of the Sixth Army has proclaimed, from now forward, the official name of the BOIS DE BELLEAU is changed to that of BOIS DE LA BRIGADE DE MARINE.*

Then Cam Abright sailed for Haiti. Like he said, he wasn't going back to no farm. He was a Marine and trouble was his business.

He figured the Germans, and even the French, might forget in time what had happened in the Wood of the Marine Brigade.

He didn't think Americans would.

The gallantry of the Marine Brigade in France gave the Corps bright new prestige, and it gave the old breed some bright new faces. Some of the 60,000-odd new recruits who came aboard during the Great War liked it well enough to stay, a leaven to the old hard-core professionalism in the ranks.

But the Corps had lost ground, in a way. Serving as part of the Army, it had gotten away from its own peculiar functions. During the hard, brilliant fighting at Belleau Wood and Soissons, amphibious warfare remained forgotten. Because the Corps had gained its highest distinction in history fighting in the 2nd Division, many officers felt that now the future lay in planning for extended land warfare, along the lines of the Army.

But a sensible number realized that to duplicate the functions of the Army would, in the long run, result in the Corps' loss of identity. They also claimed that World War I did not — as many Allied military men insisted — set the pattern for all future wars. They said that the Corps' future lay in serving as the Navy's land arm, with the mission of seizing and defending advanced bases.

Prophetic men. Fortunate the nation which has such in its service!

Because the British effort at Gallipoli had been a failure, military doctrine stressed amphibious assaults against defended shores were doomed. Perhaps they were, with the techniques of 1914-18 . . . the Corps began to seek new techniques, new doctrine.

By 1920, it had been reduced to 15,000. But new faces, new ideas were fermenting a spirit of innovation. The banana wars still beckoned; Marines went back to the Caribbean. But even banana wars can be useful.

In Nicaragua, for instance, the Marine Corps learned more than in France.

Five

Proving Ground: Nicaragua 1927

"A man can be killed just as dead in a banana war as ever in the Argonne. . . . Marine saying, reported by Colonel John W. Thomason, Jr.

As the brief tropical twilight flared redly and died in the foothills of northern Nicaragua on the evening of July 15th, 1927, the dense underbrush surrounding the little town of Ocotal was alive with more than the call of night birds.

More than six hundred heavily armed men surrounded Ocotal as the red horizon turned deep purple and night fell. In the thickening dark, a small, brown *bandido* with two pistols in his belt turned to his leader and asked, "Now, *Jefe?*"

The slender man in checkered jacket and broad Panama hat frowned. He snapped, "No, Espinosa. We wait until the *yanquis* are all sleeping — "

Espinosa smiled. He was proud to be second-in-command to a man of such genius. He looked at the thin man's deep-lined dark face, with its broad, Indian nose and pointed chin, and the long black hair cascading down from behind the Panama. The chief knew what he was doing.

The thin man thought so, too. He had an excellent intelligence service, for the peasants and *Indios* had no great love for the *Yanqui* interlopers, and they talked freely about what the foreigners were doing. Sometimes, of course, they proved more reluctant, for even the slender *jefe* had to admit the common people had also no great affection for the revolutionary army. Then it took the newfangled device the revolutionary army had learned from the old government. The bare wires from a field telephone were wrapped tightly around the recalcitrant's genitals and the phone was rung vigorously.

It was an excellent way to establish communication, indeed. Even the most stolid Indian became a font of information for the intelligence service after his number had been rung a few times.

The slender man in the checked jacket knew there were only 37 Marines in Ocotal, plus some 48 men of the local Guardia Nacional under Marine command, to face his six hundred. The war had been quiet for a long time, and many of the Marines had been withdrawn. The revolutionists needed a success now, to keep the guns and money flowing in to them, and the thin man felt the time had come to strike.

His name was Augusto Sandino, and with the exception of Fidel Castro he was the most successful guerrilla leader to appear in Latin America in the 20th Century.

He had fought as a minor lieutenant in the armies of Moncada during the palace revolution against the U.S.-supported Diaz government. When the American government sent in the Marines to establish order, Moncada had seen the handwriting on the wall and thrown in the sponge. When the 5th Marine Regiment had landed and seized the railroads, Moncada ordered his followers to surrender their arms.

Discipline in the Moncada forces was less than perfect, however. Augusto Sandino had sneered at the order, and he slipped away into the northern hills with a band of 150 men.

Sandino was an obscure man in many ways. His motives were never clear, even to those close to him. He professed love of country and hatred of the *Yanqui* invader with brilliant eloquence, and this eloquence soon rallied an army to his flag. Donations were taken for him in many countries of South America, where fear and envy of the Colossus of the North lay close to the surface in many breasts, and somehow guns and supplies reached him over the tortuous trails.

Though he amassed as many as 3,000 men, few Nicaraguan patriots rallied to his call, and there was an unmistakeable stamp of banditry about many of those who did. The legal government placed a price on his head and most of the old Moncada men refused to aid him.

But eloquence in Latin America is more important to a revolutionary general than military skill, and soon Sandino had a great following in many lands, not excluding the United States. It remains a matter of some irony that Augusto Sandino received far more support from bleeding hearts and idealists in the United States than from the peasantry of his native land.

Now, on the 15th of July, 1927, six months after the Marines had landed, Sandino held his ragged but feral guerrilla army back from Ocotal until midnight passed. Then he gave the word to Espinosa who grinned ferociously and drew his pistols.

"*Adelante, muchachos!*"

Brandishing razor-sharp machetes, waving Remington and Mauser rifles, Sandino's army rushed into the darkened streets of Ocotal.

The United States Marine Corps Guidebook states that wherever Marines are stationed, ashore or afloat, the commanding officer will establish and maintain an interior guard. Guard duty is a function of special importance to Marines since it is their duty to provide protection for all naval shore installations anywhere in the world.

At approximately 1:00 A.M., July 16th, 1927, this devotion to guard duty saved the lives of both the 37-man detachment and the men of the Nicaraguan Guardia Nacional.

"*Alto! Quien viva?* Who goes there?"

And as the dark shapes pressed forward into the streets, the orange-purple flash and sharp, ringing *spang* of a Springfield shattered the thick night. A revolutionary howled and let his rifle fall clattering on the hard-pressed earth.

The sharp-eyed sentries knew better than to yell for the corporal of the guard. Firing, they fell back on their barracks, a stone building in the center of town. The town of Ocotal exploded into continuous uproar.

Sandino's men plunged through it like maniacs, but the Marines had stood to, and in the building beside them the Nicaraguan Guards were ready. As Sandino sent his *bandidos* charging both buildings, a blast of rifle fire swept the street. The rebels faltered.

Espinosa rushed among them, screaming Spanish and Indian curse words. They reformed and approached the buildings once more. And again the steady, spiteful cracking of the Springfields killed many, drove the others back out of sight in the shadows.

Sandino was discovering the truth of General Pershing's remark in France: *The deadliest weapon in the world is a Marine with a rifle.*

The Sandinistas began to place fire of their own against the barracks, but the building was solid and their marksmanship execrable.

Against repeated charges and steady sniping, the small Marine detachment held fast. Sandino had taken Ocotal, but until he destroyed the tiny detachment that was the town's heart he had really taken nothing.

This he knew, and through the long hours the fire-fight blazed.

At dawn the Marines were still holding out, and with light their rifle marksmanship grew deadlier. Now they could see to shoot, and any Sandinista who showed himself was apt to be hit immediately.

Augusto Sandino went among his troops, shouting, urging them on with his famous eloquence. If they had had even the rudiments of military training, they might have overrun the Marine defenders by sheer numbers. But they could not organize a concerted attack, and now that simple throat-cutting seemed out of the question, many hung back.

At last Sandino ordered, "Back — back, *muchachos*, to the brush!"

The rebels pulled back from Ocotal. But Augusto Sandino was not through. He said to Espinosa, "*Oye*, we have lost nothing. We merely change tactics. The Marines are very few; they cannot break out of Ocotal and escape in the jungle. It is more than a hundred miles to Managua and the nearest *Yanqui* reinforcements. A week to get here over the trails. You understand?"

Espinosa understood. Grinning, he said, "*Si, Jefe*. We keep the town surrounded. When the Marines' ammunition is expended — " He caressed his nickel-plated revolver while Sandino nodded agreement.

As the hot morning sun sent steam up from the damp undergrowth outside Ocotal, the steady ringing of rifles sounded from around the town. Cut off and surrounded, the Marines and Guardia fought back, firing whenever the guerrilla pressure came too close.

They were in deep trouble, and they knew it.

At 10:10, July 16th, Lieutenant Hayne D. Boyden roared over Ocotal in his ancient De Haviland. He and his wingman, Gunner Michael Wodarczyk, had flown out from Managua on routine patrol to see what was happening in the foothills.

Something was going on, all right. Boyden nursed his old crate down just above the tree tops. Even above the roar of the engine he could hear a faint popping of gunfire, but the brush and town obscured his view.

He passed over the town once more, certain now that Ocotal was under attack, certain also that he had to have more information before returning to Managua.

If there were cautious men in the Marine Corps of the Nineteen Twenties, they were not in the Aviation Service. It required the antithesis of caution merely to take one of the aircraft of the period aloft. Boyden waggled his wings at Wodarczyk, then pointed down with his right hand. Wodarczyk nodded.

While Wodarczyk peeled off and flew at the jungle, firing his machine guns to keep the *bandidos* occupied, Hayne Boyden brought his DH down into a small clearing. Leaving the engine turning over, he jumped from the cockpit and set out to see what he could find out about the situation at Ocotal.

He quickly accosted a native who had come to see the strange machine and the stranger man who flew in it.

"*Que paso, hombre* — what's happening?" Boyden demanded, in passable Spanish.

The Nicaraguan, friendly to the *Americanos*, quickly filled him in.

"Damn!" Boyden said. He quickly got back into his cockpit and bumped across the field, roaring aloft.

He joined Wodarczyk, who was happily expending his machine gun ammo against the rebel-held jungle. Wodarczyk was quite a character. He flew because no law of man or the Corps could keep him on the ground. The Polish warhorse had emigrated to the States at the age of fourteen, joining the Marines when he was old enough. He had risen to gunnery sergeant in France in the war, then, seemingly unhappy at having lived through that small fracas, he had applied for aviation duty.

In the 20's the Corps accepted many enlisted men as pilots — NAPs, naval aviation pilots, they were called. NAPs were normally skilled mechanics, and in the days of temperamental, baling wire planes and haphazard ground service, few made better pilots. Most NAPs did not have the educational requirements — a degree — required for commission, but the Corps was happy to have them. It was a way to expand its aviation service without exceeding its very limited authorized officer spaces.

The old De Havilands climbed high, then peeled off again at the rifle flashes ringing the Marine garrison in Ocotal. For twenty minutes Boyden and Wodarczyk made passes at the jungle, then, their ammunition gone, they turned their crates toward home and sighed away.

Noon came to Ocotal, and in the blazing heat of midday the 37 Marines began to count their remaining rifle ammunition. The bandoleers had melted away at a frightening rate. To hold off a force the size of Sandino's they had to keep up a heavy fire, and it was inevitable that they must soon expend their last few rounds.

They had heard and seen Boyden and Wodarczyk, and had been grateful for the small help the fliers had rendered. They realized the aviators would give the alarm in Managua — but Managua was a good week's march away through the mountains and jungle.

Sweating in their faded khaki, faces grim beneath the battered campaign hats, the cut-off Marines could only fight on against impossible odds.

Sandino would get them in the end, but he wouldn't get them cheap.

At 12:30 Hayne Boyden and Mike Wodarczyk reported to Major Ross Erastus Rowell, commanding officer of VO-7M. The numerical designation of that outfit of half a dozen creaking De Havilands indicated that it was a Naval Observation Squadron. VO-7M had been constituted from the breakup of VO-1M and VO-4M, outfits which had come earlier to Nicaragua, hauling their aircraft up to Managua from the coast on railway flat cars. There they had constructed a landing field and flown valuable patrol and reconnaissance missions for the continual Marine ground patrols.

But Rusty Rowell was a man of ambition. He was not an officer to passively observe a scrap if there was any way he could take part in it. The official mission of VO-7M bothered him not at all, if he decided to do something different.

Rusty Rowell had learned to fly by paying for lessons out of his own pocket, and he had transferred to the flying service in the face of all the opposition his superiors could muster. In 1923, at the age of 39, he had received his wings.

For two years, in 1924 and 1925, Rowell had the highest bombing score in the flying service. Placing him in charge of an observation squadron was no effective way of discouraging his talents. For there were a few things Rusty Rowell had long wanted to try out.

At Kelly Field he had watched Army pilots practicing a technique, they said they had learned from the British. They called it dive bombing, but no one, not even the British, thought very highly of it. It was something to practice and to talk about — but it seemed a highly dangerous maneuver in a service already dangerous, and it received no official encouragement.

In the 1920's, Rowell knew, the military air services ran close to a twenty-five percent casualty rate from routine flights alone — a figure ground forces considered ruinous to efficiency and morale.

Since nothing short of death could hurt the morale of his flyers in VO-7, Rowell trained them in this new technique. Dangerous it was but, since it was new, they took to it like kids to candy.

Now, listening to Boyden's terse report, Rowell frowned. Those boys at Ocotal were finished unless — Rusty Rowell suddenly smiled. He had five operational De Havilands, and he had a supply of 17-pound fragmentation bombs. And every ancient DH had a jury-rigged bombing rack under its lower wing.

A slim dynamic man at 43, Rowell gave swift orders. When he finished, his four pilots were grinning, too, just as if they had good sense.

A few minutes later, five DHs roared and bumped their way across the little 400-yard runway, clawing their way painfully aloft. When the squadron was airborne, Rowell waggled his wings and pointed his nose in the direction of Ocotal.

Happily, like clumsy fox hounds in full cry, VO-7M buzzed after him.

As the day lengthened, Augusto Sandino had noted well the slackening in the *Yanquis'* fire. With darkness soon ready to close in he saw his men squatting in the shade of trees, putting a final edge to their long machetes. It was a rare Nicaraguan who ventured anywhere without his sharp machete, and it was a tool dearer to his heart than the noisy Remingtons. It was also a tool he knew how to use infinitely better than a rifle, too.

Six hundred machetes against less than a hundred bayonets — these were the kind of odds that put sparkle in a guerrilla's eye. Sandino smiled.

Espinosa was tugging at his sleeve. *"Mira — mira los aeroplanos!"*

Sandino heard the spurting, hesitant roar of the engines as they passed overhead. Mildly interested, he looked up, seeing the five bulky, clumsy shapes that circled overhead.

Espinosa stepped out into the open with many of the rebel army. They rarely got a good opportunity to see airplanes even though the Nicaraguan Air Force had bombed them on occasion. Flying two old

Laird-Swallows, the government aviators flew over them at great height, dropping capped dynamite sticks.

The *bandidos* enjoyed the performance immensely. It was like seeing fireworks, and the dynamite sticks did about the same amount of damage.

Espinosa shook his head admiringly. "The men who go up in those are *loco* — quite mad," he said. A DH dived out of the column at 1,500 feet, headed straight down. The engines roared and the air passing through the struts began to scream. The rebels stood in small knots, their faces pointed upward.

"What's this?" an officer asked Espinosa.

"He is crashing, I think," Espinosa said. "Maybe he is out of fuel."

The plane plummeted downward toward the clearing, the shriek of its descent rising to a shrill crescendo.

Slightly nervous, Sandino's men tried to pick the place where it would hit. It appeared that the plane would fall among the trees, so they did not move.

At 600 feet, Major Rowell jogged the bomb release, then pulled back on his stick. Slowly, painfully, he manhandled the nose of the DH upward. The nose lifted and the DH leveled, then whipped over the trees with a shattering roar.

Brrram! Brram! Brrram!

Fire and smoke burst among the gathered rebels gawking up into the air. Espinosa, staring upward, saw a black object hurtle toward him. It grew and grew, till it filled the sky.

With a howl he sprawled to the ground, flat on his face.

Brram!

Dirt showered him, his ears felt as if they had burst, and all around him slower rebels dropped screaming with pain. More than a dozen did not move again.

"*Chingado!*" Espinosa said. He scrambled on hands and knees toward the brush, for now four more airplanes were hurtling down out of the sky, one after another, raining death on the cowering rebels. When they climbed again, growling back to a thousand feet, the wounded screamed for aid. Others lay still in large pools of blood.

VO-7 came back with machine guns to finish the job.

The 37 Marines sallied out of Ocotal and captured Sandino's death-head flag. They counted close to 80 dead *bandidos* and estimated that nearly 200 *Sandinistas* in all had been hit by bombs or bullets.

Augusto Sandino and his remaining followers slipped away into the jungle. A man who could profit by experience, he would not attack a Marine stronghold again.

Major Rusty Rowell and his boys had launched the first low level air attack in support of ground troops. They had taught the Corps a new trade, one in which, in a later war, they would have no peer.

Now, the Marine effort was to keep a thin line of patrols and outposts between Sandino in his northern hills and the rich plantations of the southland. Sandino's intelligence service was too good for the Marines to hope to surprise him, and he would not willingly choose open battle. Nicaragua was a friendly nation, and the Marines were on her soil by agreement of the government, and repressive measures against the population, even *Sandinistas*, were out of the question.

It was the familiar pattern of guerrilla war, already old to the Marines, which would in years to come be familiar to all the world. The Marines were four years in Nicaragua and during this entire time Sandino was successful in eluding capture; and he achieved a certain success. His campaign, probably as much as anything else, led to rising Latin American insistence that the "large policy" be abandoned, and the futility of the action against Sandino led a great number of Americans to share this view.

But in the course of fighting Sandino the Marine Corps was learning new lessons, both in the air and on the ground.

PFC George Boze got his tail in a crack, along with 150 other Marines near Quilali December 30, 1927. It had been a big patrol, two columns, and Augusto Sandino figured the Marines were giving him a belated Christmas present by sending it into his country.

George hadn't had any more warning than the rest of them when the fire ripped out of the surrounding brush. Four Marines were down, dead, and eighteen others hit, including both column commanders. The loss of the officers made it bad because it delayed whatever quick action against the attack they might have made until it was too late.

Both columns were pushed back into Quilali by hundreds of skulking, sniping *Sandinistas*. There George Boze and the Marines could hold the guerrillas off because the guerrilla hadn't been born who could cross an open field of fire in the face of Marine-held Springfields.

George knew they were in a lot better shape than the 37 in Ocotal had been. In Quilali they had plenty of ammunition and supplies; they had some contact with the outside world through aircraft, and help could reach them in plenty of time. There was only one problem — the 18 wounded Marines.

The aircraft could and did drop medical supplies for them, but without surgical help some of them were going to die, and soon.

Major Rowell and his boys couldn't drive the *Sandinistas* off because they had since learned to dig holes or otherwise take cover against the small bombs and machine gun strafing.

The Marines dug in around Quilali, sniped back at the skulkers, and waited. For him and the others, that was okay, George Boze thought; they had time. He had joined the Corps more than anything else to see the world, something he hadn't seen much of as a grocery clerk in Washington State. But he was 22, and he had time. It was only the wounded who didn't have time.

He was oiling his rifle against the humid air when Sergeant Brannan picked him and a couple of others for a special detail.

"What's up, Sergeant?" George asked.

"Goin' to set some fires," Brannan grunted.

"What the hell? You figure I'm a pyro — some kind of fire bug?"

Brannan was gray, past forty. "I figured you was a kid at heart, Boze," he said patiently. "No, we got to burn down part of the town here. Clear a space for a plane to come in."

"Plane?" one of the others of the detail asked.

"Some idiot has volunteered to land a plane in Quilali to take off the wounded," Brannan growled. Then, realizing the idiot in question undoubtedly wore bars, he shut his mouth. "Let's go."

George squinted his eyes against the searing tropical sun and picked up his rifle. It was a fine day for a fire — hot as hell.

The burning part was fine; George got sort of a kick out of it, watching the frame buildings go up in smoke. Then, before the ashes were cool, they had to go in and level the ground. That, unfortunately, was work. But soon they had several hundred yards of ground more or less clear inside the Marine perimeter.

An O2U biplane growled low over the town, dropped a note.

"He ain't got no brakes," Sergeant Brannan said morosely. "Some of you grab his wings when the plane hits the ground and stop him."

"Oh, Jesus!" George said, aloud.

Throttling down, spurting and blowing black smoke, the new Corsair sank toward the tiny field. Lower it came, roaring, until the wheels touched down, and the biplane bounced, rushing toward the end of the cleared space at frightening speed.

George Boze and three other maniacs ran out and threw themselves across the plane's lower wing. It howled and spit and shook, but they dragged it to a halt just before it crashed into a hovel at the end of the strip.

Grinning, Lieutenant Christian Schilt threw back his oil-splattered goggles and hopped out.

Whang! Whang!

He looked in some amazement at the Marines darting away, hitting the ground.

"You're under fire, sir," Brannan called. "Them yoyos can see us from the brush!"

Schilt rubbed the grease out of his sleek young moustache and joined the rest of them on the ground.

The worst cases among the wounded were carried to the strip on litters and lifted into the Corsair. "Turn the son-of-a-bitch around," Brannan shouted. They took hold of the wings and tail, hauled the heavy plane about until it faced the way it had come. He gunned the engine, and snapped down his flying goggles.

Schilt waved a hand, and sent the biplane bumping forward over the scorched earth.

"Good luck, you silly so-and-so — sir!" George said under his breath.

The O2U shook, gathering speed. It growled — and choked and coughed, hurtling forward toward the end of the runway; then, at the last second, its wings bit the air and it went aloft with a high whine. It cleared the obstruction at the end of the runway by a scant few feet. A scattering of shots from the surrounding *bandidos* sped it on its way.

"My, God!" George Boze said aloud. He let out his breath. The pilot had been damned lucky, he thought. He could never do that again.

Some time later, George listened to desultory rifle fire on the outskirts of town as the beleagured 150 Marines held the skulking hordes at bay. He heard Corsair engines again, saw Schilt's plane circling the crude runway.

"All right, hit the deck!" Brannan called. "He's comin' in."

"Jeez, how many time's he gonna do this," George complained.

"Till all the wounded are out," the grizzled sergeant snapped.

"Now, lay hold of those wings when he hits the ground — "

Lieutenant Schilt dropped the Corsair into Quilali *nine* more times, and *nine more times* he barely cleared the runway, each flight bearing a load of wounded Marines. With the last injured man safely aloft, he waggled his wings, made the Corsair engine spurt smoke and disappeared in the direction of Ocotal.

Around the town the guerrilla war went on. In time, the *insurrectos* got a bellyful of Marine marksmanship and the war died down again.

PFC Boze had been in the service long enough to take a jaundiced look at some of the medals that were handed out. But when he heard that Lieutenant Schilt had received the Medal of Honor from President Coolidge on the White House lawn, he wasn't sure that one medal was enough.

After all, Schilt had made ten daring flights!

In February, George heard that the Polish warhorse, Mike Wodarczyk, had surprised a band of guerrillas in the open. Attacking at tree-top level, his tail half shot away by rifle fire, the enlisted pilot dropped his bombs at the last possible instant. Among the *bandido* dead was Sandino's *segundo*, Espinosa. For this, and after twenty-five combat missions, the Corps decided Wodarczyk was in aviation to stay and awarded him his wings and the DFC the same day.

Six of the small group of aviators were killed in operations against the enemy. Though they operated in planes that could carry only a few hundred pounds extra weight, an average of thirty tons per week was flown across the mountains to supply the ground troops.

Yes, George thought, even after he had come to see more of the world than Nicaragua, *a man could grow right fond of Marine flyers!*

Some years after the great days in Nicaragua, when the United States was adopting the "Good Neighbor" Policy toward Latin America, and Augusto Sandino had been assassinated by one of his own countrymen, the little band of Marine fliers had time to attend the air shows springing up across the nation, and to give exhibitions of their flying skill to the public.

In 1933, Colonel Rusty Rowell and his boys flew in the National Air Races by day and lived the good old days by night. They went from Los Angeles to Chicago, and finally to the Cleveland Air Races where they thrilled the watching crowds by a daredevil show of simulated dive-bombing.

After the show, a stiff-backed man approached them and spoke in a German accent. He was Major Ernst Udet, one of the great aces from the first world war. He was most interested in the exhibition, and he was most affable.

"Ja," he remarked to the younger, admiring Marine fliers, "this is most interesting. I can see possibly some remarkable developments...."

Since the smiling major was one of the greatest living officers, no one thought his interest odd. Later, when the discussion resumed in hotel rooms and the party was in full swing, no Marine thought too much of the fact that the major talked shop at great length, and took copious notes when they described how they had dive-bombed Sandino's men at Ocotal. After all, the Germans were known to be a methodical people, with peculiar ways.

But seven years later, when the Stukas designed by one Ernst Udet were terrorizing all Europe, Rusty Rowell realized it was not only damned odd, but no coincidence.

As he said ruefully, "This was an aftermath of our dive-bombing shows wholly unanticipated."

Part Two

The Greatest Test

The early years of the Twentieth Century were good to the Marine Corps, for in the Thirties it saw the turning point of Marine history.

With the abandonment of the large policy in Latin America in 1933, the Corps was free to embark upon a new program. This same year the men who had always said the future of the Corps lay in amphibious warfare won their long battle. The Fleet Marine Force, designed for island war, was organized. Even more important, at Quantico firm, sound amphibious doctrine was being written and studied.

Because most of the amphibious operations of the past had failed, as at Gallipoli, it did not necessarily follow that the concept was wrong. But new ideas, new techniques, were needed. The Corps set out to find them.

A new manual was written. Maneuvers were held. In Florida a civilian developed a weird, amphibious tracked vehicle called an "Alligator." The Corps began to see the answers to the problems posed by a landing on a hostile beach under fire. . . .

The greatest test the Corps would face, and its greatest contribution to the nation, was to find a way to cross and secure a heavily defended beach. As British General Fuller was to say, this ability was "in all probability . . . the most far-reaching tactical innovation of the war."

By the end of the Nineteen Thirties the great test was approaching.

In 1941 the Imperial Army ruled feudal Japan and this Army had lost touch with reality. Megalomaniac, with a mystic trust in victory, the Army pushed a blindly-following peasant nation into the most destructive racial war in history.

On December 7, 1941 at Pearl Harbor, Americans learned what *bushido*, the way of the warrior, really meant.

The Imperial Japanese Navy had not wanted the war against the industrial might of the West. But to all Japanese obedience was at the apex of virtues, and within six months the Navy laid all East Asia at the Imperial generals' feet.

The Navy was a superb, modern force, relying on attack carriers at a time when most Occidental admirals still admired battleships. It had some of the finest naval aviators the world has seen, flying a plane that was matchless in 1941.

The Nippon Navy seized a wide chain of islands across the Central Pacific, forging a ring of steel to defend the conquests Japan had made. Rightly, it understood the war would be a naval one. But its conquest of Wake, at terrific loss against weak defense, showed the Japanese did not truly understand amphibious war. Nevertheless, they considered their conquests safe and secure.

By accepted techniques of 1941, they were.

On the defensive, America stopped Japan's westward thrust at Midway. But to the south, Japan still held the initiative. Her troops invaded the Solomons, and began to build an airfield on Guadalcanal, threatening the life line to the Anzac nations.

On July 2, 1942, American leadership resolved to take the offensive in the South Pacific. Ground troops were scarce, but there were a few Marines down under. . . .

Six

Dark Island: Guadalcanal 1942

Nippon, the sacred land
Fights for the peace of the East
And the destruction of foreign powers.
Hear, you races of the earth!
Once there was Japan and many nations;
Soon there will be only Nippon.
Listen, you peoples of the world!
Shinto Hymn of the Year 1942, sung by Japanese soldiers sweeping the Pacific.

"No small part of the credit for victory must go to the men who seized and throughout the desperate days . . . held a critically situated airfield . . . it was Henderson Field . . . which made it possible to hold Guadalcanal." Isely, U.S. Marines and Amphibious War.

Out of the rosy mists of the Coral Sea, some ten degrees south of the Equator, rises the spiny, ninety-mile length of the island of Guadalcanal. In common with the other large islands of the Solomons Archipelago, of which it is a part, Guadalcanal is an accumulation of the ancient coral deposits of an undersea range, thrown up from the Pacific's floor by old volcanic action. The rough, precipitous terrain is cut by long ridges, cliffs and gullies. In addition, ages of tropical rainfall have covered Guadalcanal with one of the features most inimical to man — the rain forest.

From the sea, where the cooling winds blow over dimpled, light-blue waters Guadalcanal is beautiful. Its rugged peaks rise out of lush, blue-green jungle, disappearing into the misty clouds in a riot of warm, pastel color. Fringing the warm shores of the glass-clear ocean are row after row of ordered stately coco palms, for copra plantations dot the coast. To all outward appearances Guadalcanal is a paradise.

But beyond the narrow strips of coconut trees two hundred inches of rain fall each year, and Guadalcanal is pure hell. In the rain forest man — even primitive man — does not live.

Immense hardwoods claw their way up from the morass of the jungle floor, rising a hundred feet and more to blot out the tropical sun. Around the gigantic holes vegetation runs wild — vines, creepers, ferns, and impenetrable brush. In the branches of the hardwoods a few birds dwell — loud, raucous and brilliantly plumaged. What lives below is mostly loathsome.

There are rats, and lizards three feet long. There are a few snakes. In the black, still swamps and turgid rivers, scaly crocodiles — the deadly Asian crocodile — lay in wait. But the animal and reptile kingdom do not thrive in the rain forest; it is the domain of the insect world.

Huge, hairy spiders cling to rotting branches. Wasps three inches long buzz through the incredibly hot, humid air where no breeze has ever reached. Ants, whose bite is a touch of fire, swarm freely in company with scorpions and centipedes. Hungry leeches lurk in trees, waiting for a victim to pass below. Black, angry mosquitoes, carrying tropical death, move in clouds.

The earth itself is black and foul, never drying out. It steams slowly, sending up dank, sour odors. The smell of decay, of death, is everywhere.

Guadalcanal resembles the rain forest everywhere — in the other Solomons, New Guinea, Africa, South America. It is a veritable green hell.

But on Guadalcanal there is one difference. In the northeast, back from Lunga Point, there is a level area, open and topped with six-foot *kunai* grass. This area, the Lunga Plain, made Guadalcanal useful to a powerful navy moving southward toward Australia in early 1942,

Here, in early summer, the Japanese Navy built an airfield to house its deadly Zeros. By August, the runways were almost completed. Soon the planes would come down from the great bastion at Rabaul and, inevitably, another area of the South Pacific would come under the banner of the Rising Sun.

Who held Guadalcanal and its vital airfield held the lifeline to the countries Down Under.

But here, also, on August 7, 1942, the 1st Marine Division landed.

Colonel Clifton Cates, commanding the 1st Marine Regiment, watched his boys disappear into the green hell behind the coconut palms, pushing toward the Jap airfield. His Roman-nosed face under its deeply-indented forehead was worried.

When the 1st Marines, who with the 5th and Pedro del Valle's 11th Artillery Regiment formed the Division, had been sent overseas they had been told they would see no combat until early 1943. The ranks were filled with teenagers and they needed training. The 1st Marines had never held a single regimental exercise.

Clifton Cates looked at the old '03 rifles in the hands of his youngsters, watched the ancient French 75's of Del Valle's 11th Marines being sweated ashore. With this same equipment Clifton Cates had stormed Belleau Wood twenty-four years before. Only then there had been more of it, and it was equal to what the Germans had.

Nobody had any idea what the Japs possessed. All Cates knew was that they had overrun the Philippines, swamped the British in Malaya and conquered the entire East. On land they had never been stopped.

Luckily, surprise had been complete. The Japs had not tried to fight; they had departed hastily into the mountains, leaving behind the intact airfield, their cooking pots and large quantities of food.

In the jungle surrounding the field the 1st Marines had come apart. Surprised by the awful terrain, they had gotten lost in the brush, fired at shadows, shouted and yelled to each other as they crashed along. They were nervous, undisciplined, feeling a definite uneasiness at the prospect of meeting the mysterious Japanese foe.

Fear of the unknown is usually the hardest enemy to conquer.

They took Lunga Airfield, which they renamed Henderson after the squadron leader killed at Midway, because the Japanese were few, and these had orders not to fight.

Around the field the Division threw up a defensive perimeter. There were not enough men to man it adequately at a safe distance, but the beach side was heavily fortified against a Jap counter-landing. The south, or island side of the field pressed against jungle and mountains, and seemed unsuited for an attack; this they covered with scattered strong points.

On the east, they threw out a flank to the sluggish Tenaru River — actually, the Ilu, but their maps were wrong — 3,000 yards away, and to the west they dug in on the forward slopes of a grassy, open ridge two miles short of the Matanikau.

While they dug in, Jap planes came down from Rabaul and bombed hell out of them and the fleet offshore. There were Japs on the island, lurking in the jungles, and more would be coming. The Japs, would not — could not — let Guadalcanal go without a fight.

The night after they took Henderson Field and began to prepare for the American planes that would come — someday — the Marines heard heavy firing offshore, out toward Savo Island. It didn't mean much to the men in the ranks peering anxiously into the rainy night, looking for Japs.

They didn't know that an enemy cruiser had sunk four-fifths of their convoy escort, or that the screening American carriers had been forced to steam away, leaving them unprotected. Or that with the coming of dawn, the convoy, vulnerable now, would weigh anchor and depart — carrying away seventy-five percent of their yet unloaded supplies.

Colonel Clifton Cates, an old hand, knew his boys weren't ready for action as he watched them flounder through the jungles of the island. He was thinking, watching them dig in along the mouth of the Tenaru, *They've had only three months' battalion training.*

Then he thought, *Maybe we can make it up in guts.*

One of Colonel Cates' Marines was Stanley Wishka. He had been born Stanislaus, but one of the first things he'd done as soon as he was old enough was to get that changed. The other thing was to join the United States Marines.

His pop had told him, "Stanislaus, a smart man does not become a soldier. A smart man does not seek trouble."

And Stan had said, "I don't want to be no soldier. I want to be a Marine." He didn't say that 'no smart man went down in the coal mines, either,' because Pop was from the old country and he didn't take that kind of talk.

After Pearl Harbor, Pop, and even Mom, quit fussing about it.

Now, leaning back against the wet sand of his foxhole beside the Tenaru, wishing he could keep the rain from running down his pants, he was listening to Buddy Carmichael with one ear, while his blond, big-chinned face pointed across the dark water, watching the coconut palms over there.

Buddy, squat and freckle-faced, was saying, "Hell, we done our job. We knocked off a beachhead and the airfield. The rest is up to the Army."

"Sure," Joe Mecklin agreed. Mecklin was tall and thin, and although he was only nineteen, most of his sandy hair was gone. "I bet they got the Army on the way now. It's just a matter of holding here a few days — "

"Where do you think they'll send us, Joe?" Stan asked, not taking his eyes from the grove over there. He figured they shouldn't be talking, but hell, everyone was talking all up and down the line.

Carmichael butted in. "New Zealand — I got the word."

"Yeah?"

"Sure, heard it at the CP. Hey, that New Zealand's quite a place. I hear those women down there'll do anything for a Yank."

"You hear how long we'll be here?"

"Yep. Not more'n three weeks at the most."

They heard airplanes circling Henderson Field. They looked back over their shoulders, saw the yellow-white flares pop high in the air. "Here comes Louie the Louse — "

When the Louse had completely lighted the field, Washing Machine Charlie buzzed over, dropping a stick of bombs. Every night he came down from Rabaul, just as almost every night the Jap destroyers stood in off Lunga Point and shelled the beachhead.

"Oh, crap," Carmichael said. "No sleep tonight!"

Stan, miserable and wet, his face afire from mosquito bites, stared back into the silent, fearful jungle. He was hungry — they only got two meals a day since the supply ships had steamed away.

He thought, *I wish I was fighting the lousy Germans. He hated Germans, particularly Nazis.* Japs gave him the creeps.

During the entire first week on Guadalcanal, Colonel Frank B. Goettge, Division D-2 — Intelligence Officer — had been unable to get any information concerning the enemy. The Japs lurked in the heavy jungle; they did not fight; they did not show themselves. A few Korean laborers had surrendered; they didn't know anything concrete about their former masters.

Understandably, when a patrol brought in a wounded Jap, Colonel Goettge pounced on the prisoner like a tiger.

Through an interpreter Goettge learned there were Japanese troops west of the Matanikau. They were in a bad way — short on rations, riddled with sickness and without medicine. At least, that was what the interpreter thought the Jap was saying.

Goettge saw a chance to induce the enemy to surrender. Perhaps, if he made contact, took a doctor along, offered food and medicines — it seemed worth a chance.

Colonel Goettge, in common with most American officers in 1942, knew absolutely nothing about Japanese psychology.

He told the commanding general, "Let me take a patrol up there, with interpreters and a surgeon. Maybe I can make contact."

Nobody liked the idea. But Frank Goettge was stubborn. He argued, "Look, the way to get intelligence about the enemy is to go where the enemy is — "

He got his way, finally. A weirdly constituted patrol — for the mission was as much humanitarian as military — piled into a Higgins boat at night, to cruise up the beach and land in the indicated Jap area. Goettge took a surgeon, two other officers and twenty-one enlisted men, including most of his Intelligence personnel.

Splitting the night with the roar of their boat engine, the patrol shoved off. West of the Matanikau River, the Higgins boat sputtered up and down the coast, looking for a likely place to go ashore. Finally, the now thoroughly alarmed POW, who had been brought along, indicated a spot.

The boat went in. The patrol piled out, looking nervously at the dark, ominously quiet jungle beyond.

The POW didn't want to go inland.

"Nonsense," Frank Goettge said firmly. With the Jap in front of him, he pushed ahead into the thick trees, the patrol stringing out behind him.

Thump-thump-thump! Bam-bam! Spang!

The jungle blazed orange-purple streaks of fire. High in the trees the startled night birds squalled. Colonel Goettge fell dead across the riddled body of his equally dead pow.

Under a storm of small arms fire the patrol survivor's ran for the open beach. But they were surrounded on both sides by overwhelming force. On the beach they were pinned down.

They didn't know the terrain, and in the dark they were lost. The captain now in charge sent a sergeant dashing down the beach to try to reach the division's lines and bring help.

As soon as the sergeant disappeared, the huddled patrol heard a roar of firing in the direction in which he had gone. The captain, fearing the Japanese had killed him, sent a corporal on the same errand. Both got through — but not in time to do the patrol any good.

The unequal fight blazed the remainder of the night. With dawn the enemy started to close in. Almost every man on the beach was wounded. The surgeon crawled about, trying to do what he could. A bullet smashed him down, his blood staining the deeper red of the cross on his armband.

The Japs rushed forward. A couple of the men, badly hurt, tried to hold up their hands. Howling, the Japanese bayonetted them or shot them where they lay.

One Marine, the only man not too badly wounded to swim, broke away and plunged into the surf. Under a hail of bullets, he swam past the Jap-held beach and miraculously reached safety.

PFC Stanley Wishka saw the bleeding, exhausted man when he returned to the 1st Division. He heard the story of Goettge's patrol and he forgot about the Germans. A sudden, fierce anger seared his heart.

Colonel Goettge, not understanding the enemy, had made a foolish mistake. He had cost the Division four good officers, including a fine surgeon, and key enlisted personnel. But, in a fashion, he had accomplished what he had set out to do: the Division had gained some information about the enemy.

The Marines had learned what kind of a war this was going to be.

Colonel Ichiki Kiyono — or, in Western fashion, Kiyono Ichiki — had been scheduled to lead his 900-man force onto the beaches of Midway. But fate and the U. S. Navy had denied him his chance to die for the Tenno, for the Japanese invasion fleet had never reached that island.

Waiting on Guam, Kiyono Ichiki knew he would get a new chance. A great many Americans would have to be exterminated before the triumphant soldiers of *Dai Nippon* landed on the shores of California.

A clear-skinned, slender-handed man, with the dark eyes and straight black hair of his race, Kiyono Ichiki held to Shintoism. He worshipped the Chrysanthemum, the mystic symbol of the God-

Emperor and the God-State. And he was influenced deeply, as were most people of his class, by Zen Buddhism. He believed completely in the power of the inner spirit to prevail.

The *Gumbatsu*, the ruling military clique, were convinced Nippon must conquer; her disciplined spiritual power, her belief in victory was so superior to the crass materialism of the foreigner.

Kiyono Ichiki had never heard the words: *Put your trust in God, boys, but keep your powder dry.* Had he, he would have smiled or sneered. Such a Western concept was alien to his thinking.

Reality, after all, was what Kiyono's strength of spirit made it. In this trait, carried to the realms of self-delusion by upperclass Japanese, Ichiki was as incomprehensible to Western minds as they were to him.

Now his orders came. The insolent foreigners had dared to land on Guadalcanal, an island of the Solomons, and seize an Imperial Navy air base. From Guam to powerful Truk, the great, mysterious Japanese naval base, and from Truk down the Slot on six sleek, swift destroyers sailed the Ichiki Force. After dark on August 18, they splashed ashore east of Lunga Point. On land, Colonel Ichiki gathered his splendidly-equipped force behind the banner of the Rising Sun, and he did not condescend to wait for his artillery to be put ashore.

He led his troops westward toward the mouth of the Tenaru, which met the sea only 3,000 yards from the air field. The mouth of the tidal river was blocked by a little sand spit, forming a land bridge to the west.

Kiyono Ichiki did not know how many Marines opposed him; he did not greatly care. Marines were believed to be inferior in spirit, and thus in fighting ability. He did not arrange for the dominant Imperial Navy offshore to support him by fire. He did not even inform his waiting assault troops where they were, or whom they fought.

The men in the ranks, waiting in the jungle for night to fall, figured they had landed on Catalina Island, off the coast of California.

While the Ichiki Force gathered behind the coconut palms east of the Tenaru and the sun sank westward, the carrier *Long Island*, two hundred miles southeast of Guadalcanal, turned slowly into the wind. Closer to the dangerous island she dared not come — but she could send help.

Henderson Field was ready to fulfill its mission. One by one, the Marine aircraft of MAG-23 roared off the sloping decks of the carrier, droning away westward into the hazy, tropical mists. Nineteen solid F4Fs, Grumman fighters, and twelve SBDs, Douglas Torpedo-bombers, departed-the *Long Island* for their new home.

As they swooped low over Henderson Field, shaking the palm fronds, the Marines on the ground shouted and threw helmets in the air. Some men cried. Even Colonel Clifton Cates, the battle-hardened commander of the 1st Marines, felt his eyes blurring.

These planes, and those which would come after them, would save the island — if the ground Marines could hold Henderson Field.

Waiting in their damp holes, Stanley Wishka, Carmichael and Mecklin knew something was up. The day before a patrol had hit a Jap detachment moving toward the river, and the dead Nips they examined wore clean, fresh uniforms; they carried rifles without a speck of rust. Obviously, they had not been long on Guadalcanal.

And obviously the enemy had been reinforced. Lieutenant Colonel Pollock, the Marine battalion commander, had come along the line, telling the men to stay alert.

Down by the mouth of the river, where the sand spit made it easy to cross, the 1st Marines put the bulk of their defense, along with two platoons of the Special Weapons Battalion, so that automatic weapons fire could sweep the sands.

They had even found some rusty barbed wire in an old copra plantation fence. This they strung in front of their positions as a makeshift; their own tactical wire had departed with the convoy.

Across the river the birds screamed and squawked, and the crabs scuttling across the beach made eerie sounds.

We're in for it, Stan Wishka was thinking. Them Japs are supposed to be the best jungle fighters in the world. Jeez, I wish I was fighting the lousy Nazis —

It was past midnight, and his dungaree jacket was wet with sweat. He slapped a mosquito and shifted his rifle to cover the river.

There was no warning. There was only a sudden, shrieking rush of howling men out of the coco palms across the river — dark little forms holding long, bayonetted rifles — racing across the sand spit.

"Jesus H. Keerist," Buddy Carmichael said, almost reverently, in the hole next to Stan. Startled, Carmichael did not even lift his rifle.

But the night exploded into flame and shining steel as other trigger fingers tightened spasmodically.

Bucabucabuckl Bucabucabuckl Bam-bam-bam! Thump-thump-thump!
The slow, deep-throated roar of the heavy thirties slammed the night. The BARs thumped crazily, making sand and water spurt high. The short, angry Reising guns clawed the dark, stopping only when they jammed. Punctuating all the automatic weapons, Marine 03s went off like Chinese firecrackers.

Screaming, the first wave of Japanese went down. The second wave smashed across the bleeding bodies, running into the same fire.

Spang! Spang! Spang!

Working his bolt frantically, Stan fired into the howling mob only a few yards away. Then, his fingers shaking, he fumbled for a new clip, jammed it into the Springfield's magazine and shot the bolt home. The screaming attack had him shaking, but he leveled the rifle, blasting another Jap back onto the sand. He fired seven more rounds into the mass of charging fresh, saw it melt away into the shallow water.

The third wave reached the rusty barb wire. There it stopped, screaming and howling in rage and frustration while the Marine guns tore it to bleeding, silent dead flesh.

Slamming a fresh clip home, Stan found his fingers had stopped shaking. Raising the 03 to his shoulder, he killed a Jap trying to crawl under the wire. Somewhere in the back of his mind a cold, clear, steadying thought took hold of him: *This is stupid.*

From across the river, the enemy screamed and hollered — *"You die, Marine! You die, Marine!"* The screams and taunts echoed weirdly through the jungle.

It made Stan's flesh creep — but if the bastards thought they could scare him to death, they were nuts.

Despite the ferocity of the Marine barrage, the enemy kept coming. The mouth of the river was choked with dead and dying Japanese, but still more clambered across the corpses of their companions.

A few made it through the wire, raged among the Marine foxholes. A big Jap sergeant hurled a grenade toward Carmichael's hole. *Blam!*

Carmichael fell forward across his rifle.

Stan swiveled, firing the 03 sidewise in his hands. He blew the charging Jap off his feet. The few others who had reached the holes quickly died. But they had drawn blood. Carmichael was dead and others were critically wounded.

With loud wails, a fresh charge of Japanese was piling up against the wire. Mercilessly, the Marine machine guns went to work.

When the eastern sky turned red with the tropical dawn, there was more blood than water in the mouth of the Tenaru. The sand spit looked like a fresh abattoir.

The tide came in, washing sand over the sightless eyes of the corpses, filling their gaping mouths with sand.

And still the fire fight went on, for across the river Colonel Ichiki would not withdraw. His survivors huddled among the palm trees, firing with rifles and mortars. Kiyono Ichiki was learning the hard way that a conquering inner spirit cannot prevail over men of equal spirit who also know how to shoot.

Colonel Del Valle's field guns opened up, churning the Jap, positions. And with a screaming roar, down from the heavens dived the prettiest sight Stan Wishka was ever to see — Marine planes, guns blazing in close support of the riflemen.

The battle could only have one end. While the 2nd Battalion of the 1st Marines pinned Ichiki's men down from across the river, the 1st Battalion flanked across the Tenaru a mile upstream and took the Japs in the rear.

The only thing the Marine officers could not understand was this: what in hell was the enemy up to? The Jap tactics made no sense to the veteran Marine commanders. They did not have, nor would they ever have, a clear understanding of the mind of Kiyono Ichiki and his kind.

Soon screaming, shell-shocked Japs ran from the coco palms, plunged into the surf. Remembering Goettge's patrol, Stan and the men beside him steadied down, took careful aim before cutting loose with their weapons. It was like being on the rifle range.

Then a platoon of light tanks clanked across the sand spit to finish off the remaining men of Ichiki Force. Behind them spread out Stan and a thin wave of green-clad Marines.

In Colonel Kiyono Ichiki's brain the lust of battle and the death wish struggled for domination as the Marines ground closer to his position in the trees. At last, the death wish won. He put a match to the silken banner of *Dai Nippon*, watched that sacred symbol burn to ash. Then he took out his pistol and with a wild shout, put a bullet through his brain.

He had made a vow to die for the Emperor. To a man of his training, whether his death was of any practical use or not to the Emperor made no difference.

Stepping carefully across the heaps of already decomposing dead, Stan and Mecklin approached Colonel Ichiki's body warily. It was very clear what had happened.

The dead piled high on the sand spit had been bad, but here inside the palms the carnage was worse. The shelling had torn men to pieces — arms, legs, fragments of flesh were plastered to tree stumps or lying under clouds of flies on the sand.

You die, Marine, they had screamed — but it was the enemy who had done most of the dying.

Joe Mecklin put his rifle against a tree stump and quietly vomited. Behind him more Marines crossed the spit and began to pull the entrenching tools eagerly from the packs of the dead Japanese. Their own shovels, for the most part, had sailed away with the supply convoy.

Standing beside Colonel Ichiki's body, Stan took out a cigarette. It was Japanese, one of those captured at the air field; his own were used up. He looked down at Ichiki as he lit it. The slender Japanese's corpse was turning a bright lemon color in the tropic heat, a peculiarity of his race.

Stan took a drag, and it tasted pretty bad. But he felt pretty good. He had a feeling this battle was just beginning. More Japs and still more would come down the Slot, and boil up from the jungle in shrieking waves; the battle for this pestilential hell hole would go on for months until the Navy could once again establish its supremacy at sea and in the air.

It would get a hell of a lot worse on Guadalcanal before it got better.

Stan's head was a little light; maybe he was coming down with malaria. Or maybe it was fatigue. He didn't know. He didn't particularly care. He looked down at Colonel Ichiki's sprawled body again. *These guys are nuts*, he told himself.

In the awful eerie depths of the rain forest he had got the wind up over these Japs. The unknown always scared you until you faced it.

Now, Stanley Wishka figured, maybe there would be whispers running through the Imperial Army about a dark island of death far to the south where men had gone and not returned. Maybe the Japs would hear about the American butchers of Guadalcanal, and maybe a little shudder of apprehension would run through the armies of *Dai Nippon*.

He hoped so.

As for himself, and the rest of the Marines, they would never be quite so scared of this enemy, ever again.

After Guadalcanal both hatred and a certain lack of respect for the enemy seared the Marine Corps. The Japanese weren't supermen but they were bastards to fight.

Guadalcanal was the graveyard of Japanese hopes in the Pacific. For them it would henceforward be a defensive war. If America wanted to take back Japan's ill-gotten East Asia Co-Prosperity Sphere, it would have to be over the bodies of America's dead.

Now Japan's hope was to wear America down and hope for a negotiated peace.

It was a false hope. At Pearl Harbor, on Guadalcanal, at Bataan, Japan had waged a war to the knife. This she would get in return.

During 1943, after the Guadalcanal operation had ended with the United States forces in complete control, the Army bore most of the brunt of the war in the South Pacific. Fighting in the rain forests of New Guinea and the Solomons, progress was agonizingly slow.

American planners by now realized this would be an amphibious war, and that America's best and quickest hope of success lay in a smash across the Central Pacific. Japanese forces in the Southwest Pacific which could not easily be destroyed would be neutralized and bypassed.

But the crucial islands and atolls of the Central Pacific could not be bypassed. The Navy and the Army Air Forces needed them for bases in the ever tightening ring of steel they would draw about Japan.

Here, there was work again for the Marines.

Seven

Bitter Lesson: Tarawa 1943

"The one thing that won this battle was the supreme courage of the Marines who kept coming ashore in spite of the enemy's machine gun fire . . ." Major General Julian C. Smith, Commanding General, 2nd Marine Division, Betio.

In the British Gilberts, lying along the Equator just west of the International Date Line, rise the slimy barrier reefs of a coral atoll. Basically this atoll is like all others in the tropical seas. It has a deep, central, cobalt lagoon, enclosed by the jagged coral of the reefs. Around the lagoon small bits and pieces of solid land have evolved over the years and upon their surfaces coconut palms have taken root.

To this atoll, called Tarawa, came the Imperial Japanese Navy in 1942. On its principal bit of land, Betio, they built three air strips.

Betio itself resembles a dead bird lying on its back. A promontory in the west is the bird's beak; the long curve of the island to the east is its tail. The five-hundred-yard-long Burns Philip Company pier, reaching from the island to the edge of the barrier reef almost in its center, are the bird's legs, completing the illusion.

Betio is small, somewhat less than a square mile in area. It is smaller than Central Park in New York City.

On Betio the Imperial Japanese Navy unloaded many things: eight inch coast defense guns, 7.7cm rifles. They brought in great, black

13mm machine guns by the dozen. To man the guns, they imported four thousand green-clad troops of the Naval Special Landing Forces, whom Americans knew as Imperial Marines, under a rear admiral. These were hand-picked men, big for Japanese, carrying heavy .303 naval issue rifles.

The Japanese Navy fortified Betio. They had plenty of time and Japanese know how to work. How well they fortified the island the American task force standing off Tarawa Atoll November 21, 1943 would have to learn the hard way.

It would be a bitter lesson.

The American task force commander, Admiral Hill, was very sanguine about the effect of naval gunfire. He told the officers of the 2nd Marine Division, who would assault the beaches of Betio, "We do not intend to neutralize this island; we do not intend to destroy it. Gentlemen, we will obliterate it!"

A few of the Marine officers, Colonel Dave Shoup of the 2nd Marines and Colonel Mike Edson for two, were a little less optimistic. They were in no position to correct lean, handsome Harry Hill, but Edson talked a bit for the cluster of war correspondents about his transport.

Sitting hunch-shouldered, fixing them with his icy blue eyes, he said in his mild voice, "We can't count on heavy naval or air bombardment to kill all the Japs on Tarawa — or even very many of them."

Red Mike remembered the dark days of Guadalcanal when the Jap ships and planes had bombarded Henderson Field nightly. The terrific shelling had done little real damage.

He smiled as the correspondents expressed surprise. "Some of our battalion commanders think we can take it in three hours. I think it may take a bit longer. These Nips are surprising people."

The correspondents shook their heads and went away. Edson might be chief of staff of the division, and he had the Medal of Honor — but Betio Island was a piece of ground even a newsreel man could spit across in a fair wind. Under the three thousand tons of high explosive planned for the preparation fires, the damn island would likely disappear beneath the waves.

The landing was scheduled for the morning hours of November 21 because at this time the tide would be high enough to float the reef. No naval expert had, of course, stood in close enough to Betio to check, but the charts, and comparable tides in other places of the Pacific, indicated that a Higgins boat could clear the barrier reef into Tarawa's lagoon with ease.

This was quite fortunate since the 2nd Marine Division had been allotted only 75 of the new Alligator amphibious tractors. The amtracs were clumsy things compared to the faster Higgins boats, and planners preferred to use them for logistical support rather than as tactical vehicles. Just in case, however, the first three waves of Marines were scheduled to go in on the amtracs. More men than that the amphibians could not carry.

There was a New Zealand Army officer on board, a Major Holland, who kept insisting on something called "drift tides" at Tarawa — tides which held the Pacific back from the reefs at the crucial hours.

Holland was no tidal expert, of course — he didn't really know a fathom from a farthing. He was only an ex-colonial school teacher and not a practical man at all. He had only lived on Tarawa fifteen years.

Just to be sure, the Navy checked with the United States Geodetic and Survey Service — and nobody there had ever heard of a "drift tide." Of course, nobody there had ever charted the South-Central Pacific, either — but such a thing was highly unlikely.

For three days the big naval guns hammered away at the insignificant wisp of coral and sand rising out of the slimy reefs. For three days the dive bombers screamed down out of the heavens cutting loose their bombs until the surface of Betio was a shattered ruin.

Then the riflemen were served a meal of steak and eggs — an Anzac custom now a tradition in the Corps — and the transports stood in close. The Marines of the first waves went to the rails, began to climb down the slippery rope landing nets to the bobbing amtracs far below.

"Jesus," said one of the transport surgeons, a young Navy doctor, as he watched the embarkation, "that will make a nice lot of guts to have to sew up — full of steak."

PFC Barry Schilling, 8th Marines, was going in with the fifth wave. He was standing on the deck of his transport when the "obliterated" island suddenly came to life.

He could barely see the gray shape of the island lying low across the greasy-looking water in the dawn. But he saw the sudden red glare of the rocket that climbed high over the hazy coral strip.

The Japs weren't celebrating Chinese New Year. It was a signal. Ten seconds later an eight-inch shell crashed into the sea beside Barry Schilling's ship.

Whooo-oooo-oosk-barroom!

Another huge shell passed over the transport and sent a gout of water a hundred feet into the air. Steel sang across the deck; a Marine yelped, looking at a bloody arm.

Now five inch guns and 77s joined the chorus from the island. Beyond the reef the gray sea was alive with splashes.

Tarawa Atoll was not obliterated; it was not destroyed. It was about from here to Quantico short of being neutralized.

Hastily, the transports lying off the reef backed water, turned about and dashed out of range of the island guns. Behind them the small landing craft bobbed crazily in their wakes.

The big battleships of the task force turned broadside once again to Betio.

Baloom!

Sixteen inch rifles bellowed long gouts of black smoke and orange flame. In the dawn the long projectiles looked like Roman candles roaring in, leaving slow red trails in the sky. The trails arched down, hit coral. *Barroom-room-room!*

The noise bounced back across the water, struck Barry's ears like a blow. On Betio, again and again, smoke and debris spurted five hundred feet in the air.

Within minutes the island was once again in flames. Red fires burned from one end to the other, all across its eight hundred yard width. Smoke lay heavy over it. The dive bombers went in again.

And the Jap guns continued to shoot back.

Finally, the big coast defense guns were silenced. When they fired, they revealed themselves to counter battery and, one by one, they were knocked out. After a fresh half hour of battery, the naval gunners felt the island was again ready.

The first wave, already waiting in their amtracs, went in across the reef, barreling for the shore. The Scout and Sniper Platoon of the 2nd Marines, under the Hawk — Lieutenant Deane Hawkins — had already hit the pier that crossed the reef.

At 0635 the fifth wave went down into the landing boats.

Barry's sergeant, Harry Julma, called the roll in a deep voice. Julma didn't need a roster; he knew who his men were. Some of the voices that answered, *Here*, were calm, like Barry's; a few were high and tight. But every voice answered.

Barry looked at the thirty men in the Higgins boat with him. Like him, they wore a three-day stubble of beard. Fresh water for shaving aboard ship was scarce. Only Barry's dark beard was mostly fuzz. A man couldn't do much about growing a beard until he was twenty-one.

Barry's form was long and lean, still short of its full man-growth. His regular-featured, smooth face still had a boyish formlessness to it. The lines were not yet there. His brown-spotted green jungle dungarees were fresh and clean; the officers had made them change. There was less danger of infection from a bullet through clean dungarees. But already the new dungarees were slimy with sweat.

Around him the other men of his platoon — blond, sallow Koster, the fattish, short Goolsby and angry Awalt, dripped sweat, too. Heavy-bearded Sergeant Julma, took out a pair of steel-rimmed glasses and put them on. Julma wouldn't admit he needed them except when the chips were down.

"All right," Julma grated heavily. "Check your goddamn sights and windage."

The Higgins boat moved away from the side of the transport, white water breaking over its high bows, sloshing into the waist of the boat. Within two minutes every Marine aboard was sopping wet — but the water was cool. Barry Schilling was glad he had put the oil on his M-1 with a paint brush.

The Higgins boat took a long time to reach rendezvous point, where it began to circle.

From here Barry could see the island. Smoke lay over it — and something was wrong.

The boats of the fourth wave should be on those beaches now. Barry saw only a few amtracs actually on the beach. The seven hundred yard stretch from the barrier reef to the island was alive with tiny black dots — the heads of men wading in deep water.

The boats of the fourth wave were piling up on the reef. The water there was too shallow to float them.

The Navy command boat raced past the rendezvous, its officer bellowing through his megaphone: "The Higgins boats can't cross the reef! The Higgins boats can't cross the reef! You'll have to wait for amtracs to come out and ferry you — "

Waiting outside the reef, Barry saw the surface of Betio beginning to blaze with a new kind of fire — small arms and small cannon. From all parts of the island fire began to pour into the lagoon and on the landing beaches. The Japs had finally taken the wraps off their arsenal of defense weapons.

Slowly the small, clumsy amphibious tractors pulled back into the lagoon as soon as they had put the first waves ashore. Under every kind of gunfire, they crossed the reef toward the helpless Higgins assault boats waiting on the open water. The Marines would go ashore in driblets — if they went ashore at all.

Machine gun fire raved across the lagoon. Larger automatic weapons — the Jap anti-boat guns — slammed shells across the reef. Amtracs, never very many to start, were being knocked out.

One made its painful way to Barry's boat, bobbed alongside. The bearded Marine officer in its stern shouted, "All right! Fifteen of you men get aboard! Hurry up! They need help bad on the beach!"

He had said the magic words. Marines needed help! Some of their own were in deep trouble, and the men in the Higgins boat crowded forward to leap across into the amtrac.

Sergeant Julma ordered Barry, Koster and a dozen others to wait with him for the next Amphibian tractor.

Whack! Whack! Whack!

A large gun began to spank the waters around the boat. "Goddam 40mm boat gun — " Julma groaned. The coxswain put the boat hard over, sped away.

Whap!

An explosion slammed overhead with the ear-splitting crack of an air burst. Steel fragments peppered the deck; a fragment skittered between Barry's knees. For the first time he began to get scared.

The 2nd Division was a veteran outfit. All of its units had been blooded in the Solomons and it was a fortunate thing this 21 November. For the 2nd Division was going to take the highest losses in Corps history within the next twenty-four hours.

Two damaged amtracs passed passed Barry's boat; out of action, they were filled with dead and wounded Marines.

Finally, one of the clumsy tractors came alongside. "Goddamnit, hurry," Julma screamed, listening to the rising inferno of gunfire coming from Betio. "They need us in there!"

The amtrac commander shook his head. "I can't take you all the way, Sergeant — orders to keep the amtracs off the beach — too many knocked out already!"

Without the few amtracs there was no way to cross over the barrier reef. The few that were left had to be hoarded.

Moving toward Betio, the amphibian drew fire from a 77 which kept missing by inches. "Oh, Jesus!" Koster kept saying each time a round passed over.

The amtrac commander was wide-eyed with strain. "It's pure hell on the beach, men. Dead and wounded all over. Look, I can't take you farther in — you can wade from here. Okay, over the side!"

The amtrac stopped even with an old Jap hulk lying dead in the water, about two hundred yards east of the long pier.

As he went over the side into the clear, cool water, Barry heard a hail of bullets strike the side of the amtrac. He tore off his life preserver, sank neck deep in salt water. His heavy-soled boondockers scrabbled at a treacherous footing on slippery coral.

He turned toward the shore, seven hundred yards away.

Now Goolsby stepped into a hole and disappeared into deep water. He didn't come up; Goolsby had been carrying a lot of ammo.

"Shove off — shove off!" Sergeant Julma cried, wading neck deep, his hairy arms holding his oiled M-1 high over his helmeted head.

There was no time to help Goolsby.

Behind them, an amtrac took a mortar shell amidships. A chorus of screams rose up with the black greasy spurt of smoke. The amtrac sank in deep water.

Almost mouth-deep in the lagoon, the Marines could not move fast. Keeping parallel to the pier, they tried to walk erect over the slippery, sharp edged coral formations and get to the shore as quickly as possible.

It was awfully open out there on the reef, and seven hundred yards was a long way to go.

Now the machine guns found them. At least five began to fire at the bobbing heads in the water, lashing the greenish water with pink-tracered streaks of fury.

Neck deep in the surf, the Marines could not hug the comforting ground. They could not even duck. They could only stumble forward, rifles high above their pale faces.

Awalt sighed suddenly and slipped under the surface. Where he went down a thick stream of red drifted in the clearer sea water.

Harry Julma, gasped, a horrible sound. A 13mm slug had ripped his shoulder to shreds. "I'm hit!" he mumbled, thrashing, while salt water glistened from the lenses of his glasses.

There was no way to help Harry Julma. Two days later Barry saw his body lying on the beach. After two days in the water, Julma's eyes were gone . . .

The machine guns on shore sent sheets of metal into the lagoon, beating the water to reddish froth. Now there were only a half-dozen men beside Barry Schilling in the water. And they were passing the bodies of Marines of the fourth wave who had used this same route to the beach.

They took a long time to wade ashore. Seven hundred yards is a long way to go under fire. Now, nearing Betio, the water shallowed. Coral formations rose from the bottom, exposed to bright sunlight, gray and pinkish in color and smelling like something dead. A man who touched their jumbled ridges left a trail of blood.

And the shallow waters of the lagoon were littered with the bodies of thousands of dead fish. Perhaps the naval gunfire hadn't killed many Japs on Betio, but the concussion had sure raised hell with the fish.

There was still no place to hide. The machine guns rattled like grease popping in a pan. Hennessy went down, a bullet through his jaw. Fenstrum, the big blond guy who had played football and loved to brag about it, took a slug in the stomach. He fell on the sharp coral and Barry heard him moan.

You lousy sonsabitches. You couldn't hit me if I painted a red bullseye on my chest. You lousy sonsabitches!

Later, he knew he had been hysterical as he climbed up the beach, laughing and grinning at those lousy shots in the Imperial Jap Marines.

Besides himself, Koster and two others made the beach alongside him. He didn't know where the others were. Some were dead, others had cut in under the pier.

Sobbing with exertion, the four Marines splashed out of the shallow water, hurdling a half-dozen sprawled, sandy bodies lying half awash in the tide. Behind them, hundreds more steel-helmeted heads bobbed in the waters of the lagoon, making slowly for the beach.

The roar of gunfire never stopped. The enemy was throwing everything in the book at the Marines trying to cross the reef. Everything in the book was almost — but not quite — enough.

A lot of Marines were being killed. *But they weren't being stopped.*

Colonel David M. Shoup, commanding the three assault battalions, landed on the pier about 1030. Bucking the sleeting machine gun fire, he made his way ashore to take command of the beachhead.

Colonel Dave Shoup was a squat, red-faced man, bull-necked and profane. He sounded more like a gunnery sergeant than an officer and a gentleman. But under fire Dave Shoup retained complete composure, and he had one of the keenest tactical brains in the business. On that composure and tactical sense the lives of several thousand men would now depend.

Fifteen yards inland from the pier, Shoup set up his regimental command post in a hole dug in the lee of a large Jap pillbox. The pillbox was made of resilient coconut logs in several tiers and covered by several feet of hard-packed sand. The logs themselves were joined with steel. Anyone seeing this emplacement would immediately understand why the Japs on Betio had not been obliterated.

A one-ton bomb, making a direct hit, might have damaged the pillbox. It would not have completely destroyed it. And saturation bombing — or shelling — gets few direct hits.

All around Dave Shoup the beachhead was complete chaos. The beach itself was only some twenty feet wide at most points, and ended against a four-foot revetted seawall of coconut logs. Beyond the seawall Jap gun emplacements were buried, seemingly without end.

At the seawall the Marine advance had stopped.

To Dave Shoup the situation was very clear. So long as those Jap guns could fire, very little organized help could reach the men already on the beach — the first waves landed by amtrac. The succeeding waves could not be called waves by the time they reached the island, to pile up behind the low seawall. The machine guns commanding the barrier reef and the bigger Jap guns were decimating them.

Beyond the reef the movement to shore had been halted to stop the senseless slaughter. For the moment, Dave Shoup was on his own.

To Dave Shoup, the solution, also, was crystal clear. Marines had to go over the seawall and knock out the Jap guns. He began to try to push the disorganized units forward.

All the Japanese gun emplacements were underground. They were roofed with thick logs which did not burn, or with steel beams, on top of which sand or concrete had been poured. The firing apertures were small, almost invisible. From a few feet away a Jap position looked like an ordinary sand dune or a jumble of coral rock.

The positions were close together, in long lines, with interlocking fires. They were almost impossible to flank.

There was only one way the lines of emplacements could be broken. Men must charge into the teeth of the guns, knock out a pillbox with flame or demolition bombs, leaving a gap in the deadly row. Then, the others to each side of it could be approached and knocked out in turn.

There was no harder or more dangerous task in the world. It was brutal, insensitive slaughter on each side.

Colonel Dave Shoup sent the Marines forward, knowing most of the men who crossed the seawall would be killed or wounded within minutes. There was no other way. The situation would not get better.

PFC Barry Schilling and Koster were separated from their own battalion which had come ashore in driblets, leaving the reef strewn with corpses behind it. They were in with the 2nd Marines now, but that made no difference at all.

When Barry had his breath back, he sat awhile among the Marines milling around on the beach. Then he and Koster began to push their way inland. Others joined them.

They crawled over the sea wall, past men who had attacked with the first wave. A huge, six-foot Marine lay hunched in the sand, his rifle in his hand, his face lifelessly pointed toward the enemy. They crawled past him.

Within yards they passed four more dead Marines, then a dozen more. Ahead lay strands of barbed wire. Strewn through this wire were the bodies of several dozen Americans, some hanging from the barbs.

Then came a smoking pillbox, two dead Japs inside sprawled over their 13mm gun, their bodies ripped by grenade fragments. In front of the Jap position sprawled four Marines, now stiffening grotesquely into positions of death.

Several shattered amtracs lay along the beach, filled with dead Marines. Under some of them bloating bodies in green rose and fell with the gentle movement of the water.

Spang!

A Marine beside Koster collapsed, shot through the temples. His eyes gaped open in final surprise.

"There, in the pillbox — get the son of a bitch!" Koster yelled.

Barry and three others fired steadily with their M-1s. They had about as much chance of hitting the Jap sniper as the moon.

Koster lay on his back, working with some fused one quarter pound blocks of TNT. He turned over, threw the charges against the mouth of the pillbox.

Bum — Bum!

"Get that goddam Zippo up here — "

While dust and smoke boiled over the mouth of the pillbox, two men carrying the flame thrower ran forward, stopped and hunched down.

Koster threw another charge of TNT. Miraculously, this one went into the pillbox.

Bum!

Out of the swirling dust and smoke a half-naked Jap ran into the open. The sun glinted on the brass cartridges in his bandoleers.

Whoooooosh!

The flame thrower licked hotly across the coral, took the Jap head-on. He didn't have a chance to yell — he was charred instantly. The cartridges in his belt, exploding, kept the Marines pinned down for a full minute.

Then they crawled on. Ahead of them a row of dunes and rubble made noises like grease popping in a pan, and bullets tore at the earth all around them.

"Ahhh!"

Koster had caught one in the leg. Behind him the Marine with the flame thrower was also down, writhing. Barry crawled over to this man, took the weapon in his hands. He barely knew how to use a flame thrower; he had only been shown how once or twice. But he figured he could learn.

The desperate hours continued for a long time. Night came and the Marines held three hundred yards of beach, reaching nowhere more than one-hundred-fifty yards inland. They had almost as many dead and wounded as live Marines on the beach.

The Japanese might have ended it there except for one thing. The admiral commanding Betio had no communications and therefore could not organize an attack. The naval shelling had at least destroyed the Jap wire.

Colonel Shoup asked for more men. Division sent the 6th Marines ashore. They encountered the same murderous fire while plunging across the reef.

With returning daylight more Marines went over the seawall, out into the hellish charnel house of Betio. Already, the smell of the unburied dead was getting noticeable.

In Shoup's command hole, a young major reported, tears in his eyes. "Sir, my men can't advance — they're being held up by a machine gun."

"God Almighty!" Shoup shouted. "One machine gun?"

The major went back.

An officer, Lieutenant Paine, stood talking to the officers at the regimental command post. He had been out in the front of the battle more than four hours. Suddenly he collapsed, shot in the rear by a sniper.

"I'll be damned," Paine said quietly. "I stay up front for hours, then come back to the CP and get shot!"

A field grade officer was telling Colonel Shoup: "Colonel, there are a thousand goddamn Marines out there on that beach and no one will follow me across to the air strip."

One of the officers in the CP said, "I've had the same trouble. Most of them are brave men, but some are scared — "

Shoup said, almost gently, "You've got to say, 'Who'll follow me?' And if only ten follow you, that's the best you can do, but it's better than nothing."

The officer crawled away.

With curses, with sarcasm, or with gentle instruction, Dave Shoup did what he had to do. Gradually, he got the job done.

The first men who went across the seawall into the Jap inferno died. But they died violently, knocking out Japs as they fell. One by one, the emplacements were taken or destroyed.

More and more Marines came ashore until all three regiments were closing in on the narrowing Japanese portion of Betio. Tanks got ashore, and tanks were excellent pillbox crackers.

The remaining Japanese understood the end was in sight. Now, on the third night of Tarawa, they did the Marines of the 6th Regiment a favor — though it didn't look so at the time.

Company B, 1st Battalion, 6th Marines had advanced halfway down the island along the south shore, using tanks and flame throwers. At dusk they dug in at the end of the airstrip.

Here, too late and with too little, the enemy took the offensive.

"Marine, you die! Japanese drink Marine blood!"

With blood-curdling shrieks, the Jap survivors on Betio came out of their holes and threw themselves against Lieutenant Norman K. Thomas' B Company. They waved swords, bayonets, knives and grenades.

The automatic weapons chopped into the charge, but could not stop it. B Company was exhausted from a day of the most brutal combat under an equatorial sun. The night vomited Japs into the company's holes. Nevertheless, with rifle butts and bayonets the charge was beaten off.

Screaming with rage and frustration, the enemy charged again. B Company's line began to crack. Lieutenant Thomas was on the wire to Major Jones, his Battalion C.O. — "We're killing 'em as fast as they come at us but we can't hold much longer. We need reinforcements!"

Jones told him, "I haven't got reinforcements. Thomas, you've got to hold!"

A shrieking Jap leaped into Lieutenant Thomas' foxhole as he talked. Thomas tried to shoot him with his .45. It was empty. Doubling the pistol in his fist, Thomas struck the Jap in the temple, killing him.

Other Japs leaped in Marine foxholes all around. They were killed with bayonets or clubbed to death with M-1s. The B Company line dissolved into a shrieking, howling, maelstrom of demonic fury.

The Navy put down fire almost on the Marines. Marine mortars fired in support, close in to the holes. They had told Thomas and his men to hold, and they did.

There were not many of them left the next morning when 3rd Battalion moved forward to relieve them. Some were in shock; they had got through the night on sheer nerve. Cracked lips were bloody; faces of nineteen-year-olds were deeply lined. Most of the men had the thousand-yard stare. They looked at the relieving Marines and didn't see them.

But in their fashion the Nips had done the Marines a favor. Among them the butchery was fantastic. Digging them out of holes would have taken more lives than the bitter battle in the open.

With the *banzai* the Japs had shot their bolt.

PFC Barry C. Schilling, a hole in his left leg, waited on the pier for evacuation. There was no uproar now. Once in a while a rifle spanked somewhere behind on Betio, but the fight was over. It was only a matter of getting a few snipers now, like the one who had pinked Barry.

Barry shifted, reached into his filthy dungaree pockets. He had lost both his canteens during the three days on Betio, but he still had something to drink. He took out the flat half-pint brown bottle he had found in a Jap pillbox, and looked at the label. *Rare Old Island Whiskey,* the label said in English. SUNTORY. *First Born in Nippon — choicest product of Kotobukiya Ltd.*

What the hell, he thought. He took a drink, and then another. The last one was for a lot of guys who would never leave Betio.

The man-lines on Barry Schilling's face were clearly formed now. He would be shocked when he saw himself in a mirror on the hospital ship.

On the pier a lot of naval brass and other people were landing. They were coming ashore to inspect the Jap installations, to see what the Japs could do with concrete and palm logs. The party paused a moment on the pier, listening to the sound of the bulldozers digging trenches in the distance.

Then the full, horrible odor of five thousand unburied corpses crossed the lagoon and struck them. Coming in from the sea air, it was awful. The men on the island had long since ceased to mind. The newcomers began to vomit as Barry took another drink.

It was as good a way as any to drive a lesson home.

Tarawa had not been in vain. Because of the lessons learned there, on the first fully amphibious assault, thousands of Marine lives would be saved on other beaches. Without Tarawa, Saipan, Peleliu and Iwo Jima, hard as they were, would have been impossible.

The Japanese Army, once wholly *banzai*-minded, had made itself into a very capable instrument of defense.

Meanwhile, the Marine Corps continued to grow. By 1944 it had four full divisions in the field plus two unattached regiments, all veteran, and soon two more — the Fifth and Sixth — would be formed.

And the American drive toward the Rising Sun gained tempo as 1944 dawned. Now the American pattern was revealed — neutralize and by-pass all enemy holdings not essential to our advance; seize and hold and spread out from those which were. At first, it was island-hopping. It became island leap-frogging as thousands of Japanese soldiers were by-passed, left to starve on dismal islands. For now the United States controlled both sea and air in the Pacific, and ground troops on islands which she did not need could do her no harm.

Two mighty thrusts moved toward the Japanese Empire: the first, under naval control across the Central Pacific; the second, under Army General MacArthur, surged upward from the South Pacific toward the Philippines.

In the Central Pacific Marines invaded Japanese territory. There were certain islands they needed, and which they now proceeded to take.

Eight

Banzai: Saipan 1944

Tenno heika banzai! — Let us die for the Emperor!

It had been hard, bloody fighting, both for Marines and Army infantrymen on Saipan — first in the burning cane fields, heavy with the smell of charred sugar, and later in the limestone caves, sweet with the odor of death.

They had come in June 15th, 1944 on the western side of the island, catching the Japs by surprise. The Imperial Army had guessed the blow would fall in the Palaus and the Mariana defenses were incomplete.

The 2nd and 4th Marine Divisions, with the 27th New York National Guard Division, U.S. Army, came over the reefs that were ever present in the Central Pacific. But this was no Tarawa — the bitter lesson had been learned. More than 700 improved amtracs landed 8,000 men in slightly less than twenty minutes, coming in over the deadly coral with ease.

On shore it had been a more difficult proposition, Corporal Hugh N. Williams, 10th Marines, thought, as his gun crew made ready for the dawn of July 8th. The Nips had thousands of men in Saipan and plenty of artillery — the most the Americans had yet seen. There had been plenty of work for the 105s of the 10th Marines on the slow, gruelling march northward along the big island.

The Japs had been pushed back farther and farther, and the end should be in sight, Williams thought, taking out a piece of chewing tobacco. He really didn't like to chew and would in fact, have preferred a cigar. But he preferred to chew and spit, rather than having his ass shot off by a Jap sniper.

He was a calm man, a little older than most of these kid Marines in the battery. He guessed he could have been a sergeant, or higher, if he had felt like giving orders. But Hughie Williams didn't like to give anyone orders; some were cut out for that kind of thing and others weren't.

He liked the Corps and he liked the Marines around him even if they were kids. Best of all, he liked the big guns. He liked all the jobs connected with them — cutting the fuses, setting the sights or muscling the heavy projectiles into the breach. Best of all, he liked to open his mouth, stand on his toes and yank the firing lanyard — because he liked killing Japs.

After Tarawa, when he had to stand off the reef, watching the riflemen get killed because it wasn't possible to bring the big guns ashore — and after he had finally come ashore and seen the bloated bodies of Marines in the water — he liked killing Japs fine.

Looking at his lean, black-eyed face, hearing his slow speech, a man would figure Hughie Williams a quiet, placid man — the way they had figured him back home in Kentucky. A man would have been wrong. If the end was in sight, Williams wanted to get at it. He knew something was up — hell, everybody from the skipper on down knew it.

Some Jap runners had been caught with some pretty interesting messages. The Japs were calling together a big rendezvous near Makunsho Village, sending out messages to all their scattered and battered units in the line. Whatever they were going to do when they got together at Makunsho, you could bet it wouldn't be a fish fry and barn stomp.

There was movement now in the battery around him. Men were running forward to man the guns. His own crew fell in around the damp 105. He heard someone say sleepily, "Trouble north along the narrow gauge railway — the 105th Infantry's hollering for fire — "

"All right!" It was his own sergeant, tall and black in the early morning. "Let's hit it!"

"Hubba-hubba!" Hughie William muttered with doleful enthusiasm. He took his place on the squat howitzer, threw away his tobacco cud.

Maybe the Japs were starting to fry their fish.

According to the lights of *Bushido,* Lieutenant General Saito, Imperial Japanese Army, was a brave man. He had done his best to contain the American devils on the beaches of Saipan, and he had failed. He had sent messages of great victories winging through the air to Tokyo, and perhaps he can be forgiven that, for more than one commander has doctored official reports, and not only in the Imperial Japanese Army.

The Imperial Navy had promised to steam to his rescue — but the Navy had gotten involved in a battle in the Philippine Sea and had forgotten all about General Saito and the troops on Saipan.

General Saito no longer believed in promises. He no longer believed in anything except *Bushido* and the fact that he was going to die.

He decided to make the last a memorable occasion, as befitted a warrior of Nippon. But he was not going to lead the final charge. He was very old and much too infirm for that. The operation he had in mind he would leave to the capable hands of Colonel Suzuki of the 135th Imperial Infantry.

His wrinkled face sad under his iron-gray hair, Saito wrote his last message to the troops on the morning of July 6, 1944.

> *I am addressing the officers and men of the Imperial Army on Saipan . . . the barbarous attack of the enemy is being continued. We are dying without avail under the violent shelling and bombing. Whether we attack or whether we stay where we are, there is only death. However, in death there is life. We must utilize this opportunity to exalt true Japanese manhood . . . I will leave my bones on Saipan as a bulwark of the Pacific.*
>
> *As it says in the Senjinkun, "I will never suffer the disgrace of being taken alive" . . .*
>
> *Here I pray with you for the eternal life of the Emperor and for the welfare of the country, and I advance to seek out the enemy.*
>
> *Follow me!*

This message he sent out by runner to the remaining units on the island with instructions to gather at Makunsho by July 7th.

Then aged General Saito sat down to a ceremonial dinner, the best the tattered Imperial forces on Saipan could afford.

He ate canned crab meat, exquisitely prepared. There was steaming hot saki, drunk in the ritual manner, followed by a beautiful tea ceremony. A Japanese dinner can be a work of art. During the meal General Saito took formal farewell of his faithful staff.

Then, belching slightly, he knelt at the mouth of the cave which was his command post. Cross-legged, he bowed in the direction of the Emperor. Stiff-faced, his aide bowed three times, holding out the ceremonial knife.

His thin, old hands shaking, Saito put the keen steel to his belly. His parchment-like face showed no emotion. In the background of officers Saito's adjutant drew his black Nambu automatic. He knew what to do as soon as the old man had satisfied honor.

Saito's trembling hands moved convulsively, and blood spilled on the rounded, naked stomach to which he held the knife.

Blam!

The Nambu roared as the adjutant shot him through the right temple. Lieutenant General Saito had had no intention of deserting his troops. Nor had he. He had merely gone ahead, as befitted a general....

Behind Makunsho, at 0400 July 8, Colonel Suzuki gathered the remnants of the Japanese forces. Three hundred Japanese were too weak or hurt to move out. These Suzuki ordered killed, to save them the disgrace of failing to die for the Emperor.

There were three thousand able-bodied Japanese, armed with mortars, machine guns and rifles. Their officers stood in front of them, ready for Suzuki's orders. The pre-dawn gloom echoed with the clank of weapons.

Behind the organized units hobbled a procession the like of which the world had never seen. The sick and the wounded had come forth to follow Saito to glory.

There were men completely covered with bandages, men with arms and legs missing. There were men on crutches, helped along by others who were blind. Some had weapons. Some carried bayonets lashed to sticks. A few had grenades. A great many had no arms at all.

The smell of blood and bandages lay over this throng and a low moaning seemed to rise from its collective throat.

Colonel Suzuki drew his *samurai* sword, a flashing razor-sharp blade forged by an old-time master smith in the sacred isles.

Tenno Heika Banzai!

U. S. Marines in Action

The mob screamed back, *Tenno Heika Banzai!*

Then they streamed south along the narrow gauge railway toward the lines of the American Devils to follow General Saito wherever he had gone.

The outposts of the 105th Infantry, United States Army, never had a chance. Japanese attackers went through them, around them and over their bodies before their guns were empty.

Then, at 0510, the monstrous wave met the main body of the regiment. Frantic officers called for artillery; H and I Batteries of the 10th Marines did the best they could, until the wave was too close to the GI foxholes for the gunners to fire. There was no stopping men whose only concern was to die.

As dawn broke, rising out of the blue Pacific Ocean, the 105th Infantry came apart. Pockets of resistance held out here and there; others lay silent, with the men who had held them sprawled in death.

The howling, inexorable advance, its ranks thinned, continued.

Soldiers ran out of ammunition, and tried to retreat into the hills on their right. Others turned and plunged into the sea. Wading, swimming, leaving blood from their cuts on the treacherous coral, they fled across the reefs, bullets churning the water around them.

The Navy, patrolling outside the reef, rescued many of the Guardsmen. By the time the sun was up two whole battalions of infantry had disintegrated.

The Japanese wave poured on across the land to the Marine firing batteries one thousand yards behind the GI's broken lines.

"Holy Mother of God!" Joe Wodziak said as the black wave of howling demons came over the landscape toward the firing batteries. He almost dropped the fused projectile in his hands as he stared. Behind him, Hughie Williams said something wicked and profane.

He was lowering the howitzer as rapidly as the wheel would turn. Now the muzzle pointed out over the fields almost parallel to the ground.

Baloooom!

Almost at once, six howitzers vomited fire and smoke across the field.

Most of the shells went high, bursting beyond the oncoming surge of death. Artillerymen weren't used to firing at something screaming in their faces.

"Set the fuses for one hundred fifty yards!" the battery exec screamed.

"One-five-zero!" Wodziak screeched, giving the projectile nose a twist. "Cut!"

"Set!" Hughie Williams said calmly.

"Fire!"

The shells burst from the muzzles, roared through the air and seemed to explode almost at once. The rain of fragments blew great holes in the wailing wall of men. But still they came on.

Already the howitzers were reloaded with minimum charge, the fuses cut at 100. The breech blocks clicked home.

"Fire!"

Pointblank, the six howitzers flamed again and again. Torn apart, Japanese bodies littered the open ground.

After that it was no use. It was impossible to set the shells to explode any closer — the gun crews themselves would be killed.

The Jap survivors surged on, some running, some hobbling.

"Remove breech blocks!"

If the guns were lost, at least they would be useless to the enemy.

The firing blocks came out of the hot cannon. Hughie Williams pulled out his .45, Wodziak his liberated M-1. The rest of the men grabbed up their carbines.

Spang! Bam-Bam-Bam!

Williams saw a small, pot-bellied Jap officer run straight at him, a shining saber high above his head for the killing stroke.

Bam! Bam!

A miss — and another. He had never got the hang of using a handgun — and him from Kentucky, too.

Bam!

The Jap stopped, his mouth opening.

Bam!

The next shot blew him off his feet, for it hit him right in the gut.

The Japs poured into the dug-in gun emplacements in a screaming wave while the artillerymen fell back, firing with everything they had. The Japs came on — but now there weren't very many of them.

They would have wiped out Hughie Williams' gun crew, however — if the other batteries hadn't come to help. H had all it could handle next door, but here came a party of clerks, messmen, CP runners, fire direction people, firing BARs and carbines.

Wodziak was killed, a Jap bayonet slicing him open. Hugh killed a crazed, screaming Jap at three feet with his last round from the .45.

He threw the pistol in another's face, ducked as the battery clerk knocked the man over with an M-1. Then the two waves, Japs and Marines, met head-on. And the Japs were destroyed.

The Marines fought back to their guns. Somebody found the firing block. Somebody also took Wodziak's place at the fuse setter.

The howitzers began to fire at the few ragged remnants still streaming out of the dawn. In a few minutes it was all over.

But there were still more Japs along the shore.

The 23rd Marines, the 6th, the 8th and the 165th Infantry attacked the reeling remnants. That did it. The battle of Saipan was over.

That night Hugh Williams lay down beside the gun to sleep. Jap bodies were sprawled all around and they were becoming a little ripe. It would take a week to bury them all.

Wherever General Saito was, his men had gone faithfully to join him.

In the vast Pacific it was one damned island after another. Vastly superior in men and equipment now, and pressing the Japanese on all fronts, the American forces had learned how to fight the enemy. They learned which techniques worked, which did not. They began to have some understanding of the Japanese — what he could be expected to do, though they would never understand why.

But the Japanese learned, too. By late 1944 the lessons of Guadalcanal and many another island had sunk home. Slowly the *banzai*-oriented, atrociously-led medieval Imperial Japanese Army began to develop into the most skillful defensive fighters in the world.

In a war of attrition against superior forces only a fool throws his substance away rashly. All Japanese officers were not fools.

With each island, the going became tougher for the U.S. Marines. After Saipan the enemy ceased committing mass suicide. He no longer made things easy for the invader. He dug in and refused to come out. Islands could no longer be overrun in a matter of days.

It was in the stars that some day, somewhere, the United States Marines would meet Japanese fighting men almost as good as they were, under a general who would inspire the utmost respect in the breasts of Marine commanders.

As the Marines pressed ever closer to the home isles of Japan the inevitable meeting grew nearer. Finally, on Volcano Island, it happened.

Nine

Inevitable Encounter: Iwo Jima, 1945

"Victory was never in doubt ... what was in doubt, in all our minds, was whether there would be any of us left to dedicate our cemetery at the end, or whether the last Marine would die knocking out the last Japanese gun and gunner. Let the world count our crosses!" — *Major General Graves B. Erskine, Commander of the 3rd Marine Division on Iwo Jima, 1945.*

Six hundred and seventy miles south of Imperial Tokyo a small, brown, squat man in a mustard-colored uniform watched the winter winds whip long, gray, Pacific rollers on the narrow beaches of his barren island. It was a poor island, though part of the Prefecture of Tokyo itself, and one on which even frugal Japanese could barely eke out an existence.

From the few twisted pandanus trees struggling from the rock on its northern fringe to the towering mass of Suribachi Yama rising from its southern tip the island measured only five miles and less than two across. From the air it resembled a vast pork chop. Its surface was a gray and black washboard of soft rock and volcanic ash from which rose occasional wisps of hot sulphuric gases. It had newly risen from the sea and it possessed no history.

The Japanese called it Volcano Island because of Suribachi, and it was valueless — except to an invader hammering at the gates of Imperial Nippon.

The small brown man who sat atop the volcano had watched the tides of Pacific war, and he knew they raced toward his island this winter of 1945. For Volcano Island — Iwo Jima — lay athwart the main bomber route from the Marianas to Tokyo. Beneath its bleak exterior nestled the largest concentration of anti-aircraft artillery in the Empire, and from its two completed air strips angry Zeros rose to intercept the long-range B-29s winging in on the homeland, and to harass and kill the unfortunate cripples limping back from the aerial battles to the north. Its radar stations beamed early warning to the home isles. Because of it thousands of American airmen were dying.

Volcano Island, both to Japanese and invader, was beyond price. The little man knew that the American planners wanted his island, knew the blow must fall, and he knew almost to the day when it would come. But he was not unduly worried. He had a plan.

The little man was a lieutenant general in the Imperial Japanese Army and his name was Tadamichi Kuribayashi. He had a protuberant, soft little belly and a round head — and unfortunately for the United States Marines the soft belly was full of fighting spirit and the round head contained the hardest tactical brain Americans would ever meet in this war. No man better served his nation and his Emperor than Tadamichi Kuribayashi.

He was a martinet and he was a cold realist. He asked for certain things from Tokyo and, while the enemy fleets were yet distant, he got them.

Twenty-three thousand first class troops — all the island could maintain — crowded the waterless waste. Guns he had in profusion — from 50mm knee mortars to huge 320mm monsters. He had 8-inch rockets and five AT battalions. He had vastly more than American intelligence dreamed.

He knew his island. His men said, not as a joke, that if a certain hole made by a rat were mentioned Tadamichi Kuribayashi knew its location.

Discipline he understood. There were no comfort girls on Volcano Island, and the few *saki* bottles were empty, to be used as booby traps. The troops were given no time to brood on this cheerless place. Day and night they were occupied — digging.

Volcanic ash mixed well with cement to form superior concrete. Every gun, every rifle pit on Volcano Island was placed beneath the surface of the earth, and it was concrete-lined. Steel doors were fitted over cave mouths, to be rolled away when the time came. Deep, reinforced tunnels connected much of the island, from one command post to another.

Men who saw it later said no similar area of the earth's surface was ever equally fortified.

Nor did Lieutenant General Kuribayashi neglect morale and training. He knew well that his soldiers would die willingly for the Emperor, but they must die well. In each rifle pit, in each concrete bunker, was posted a mimeographed copy of Kuribayashi's Courageous Battle Vows:

Above all, we dedicate ourselves to the defense of this island . . .
We shall infiltrate into the midst of the enemy and annihilate him . . .
Each man will make it his duty to kill ten of the enemy before dying . . .
Until we are destroyed to the last man, we shall kill the enemy.

For Tadamichi Kuribayashi had a plan. He would allow the American Marines to walk into a trap . . .

Now, on February 16th, 1945, as he had known they would, the great gray American battleships rose out of the mist off Volcano Island, and their huge rifles lifted and steadied on Kuribayashi's island. With a noise out of hell itself, the monstrous projectiles screamed over the long rollers to smash against the barren lava. They would fire and fire and then, finally, would come the advancing waves of United States Marines to take and secure Kuribayashi's island.

For three whole days they fired while Kuribayashi and his men waited, safe in the bowels of Iwo Jima. The irresistible tide was lapping at the shores of an immovable object.

Deep in his command bunker near Kitano Point, Tadamichi Kuribayashi waited for the blow to fall. He had done all he could reasonably do. He was content now to leave the rest to the gods of war.

At forty minutes past six, February 19, 1945, a half hour before dawn, ten thousand assault troops from the 4th and 5th Marine Divisions were in their amtracs, running with the tide, thirty minutes' time from the narrow beaches of southeastern Iwo Jima. It was going to be a good, clear day and the water would be calm. A small assault group from Headquarters Platoon, A Company, 28th Marines, who would go in on the extreme left flank, nodded to each other and agreed they had got a break.

It was the only break they were to get for the next thirty-six days.

In the group was Billy Farrel, the company armorer. He was a three-stripe sergeant and a technician, but in the 28th Marines there were no noncombatants this 19th day of February.

He had volunteered to carry a heavy Ronson flame thrower upon his broad back. As the Alligator idled, waiting for the final neutralizing fires to end, Billy Farrel turned his weathered young face with its wide nose and alert, narrow dark eyes toward land. As with most of the men around him it was his first combat, and he wondered briefly how he would do. But he was a tough-minded man of twenty-two from the brush country of the Texas border and under his thick, almost coarse black hair his Indian-face was calm.

In the amtrac with him were Captain Wilkerson, the tall and scholarly skipper, and other men of Farrel's team — Andrew Carter, PFC, a bazooka man from Paducah, Kentucky; Gaugeler, the satchel charge carrier from Chicago; the big ex-footballer Tabert, from Fresno, with the other flame thrower; and his assistant, Hardy.

In a parallel amtrac rode olive-skinned, handsome PFC Tony Stein, cradling his home-made Stinger — an air-cooled .30 caliber machine gun fitted to a rifle stock — and tall, wiry Sergeant Schultz from the hills of Tennessee, whose heavy beard already showed black against his fresh-shaven face. All of their eyes were on the shore, for they were going in with the fist wave.

Their mission, and that of the 28th Marines, was to land, cut across the narrow southern neck of the island, then surround and secure Mt. Suribachi.

What would happen to them in the following days would be neither more nor less than what happened to the other thousands who landed on Iwo. They would do well, and more than well. Exceptional valor would become so common as to be overlooked. But the story of one assault group from A Company, 28th Marines, tells the tale of Iwo as well as any.

Now, in the murky light, twenty-six mighty warships steamed parallel to the brief hump of lava rising out of the Pacific, belching noise and destruction from the mouths of their tremendous rifles. Powerful

U. S. Marines in Action

Idaho, old *Texas,* followed by the *Nevada* and the *New York* sent shell after shell shrieking into the small expanse of exposed island until black smoke obscured the view of the men waiting in the amphibians. The *Vicksburg,* leading the cruisers, raced close, blasting pin-point targets. Secondary batteries and AA guns filled the air with steel and tracer. Destroyers in the boat lanes blazed away at the beaches with flat trajectory fire, while dozens of rocket and mortar boats made the dawn blacker with high angle missiles.

Vast Suribachi, long extinct, seemed to move and come alive under the horrendous pounding. A final flight of planes screamed low over the landing beaches, guns chattering, black bombs whining down to burst redly in the reeking sand.

It was 0830 and, with a perfectly executed maneuver, the first sixty-eight amtracs turned in toward the shore. Their engines raced, and slowly, steadily, the bows took a bone in their teeth.

Sergeant Billy Farrel, crouching low behind the armor plating, shifted the heavy flame thrower on his back. All around him heads with the camouflage-draped steel helmets bobbed; men adjusted combat packs, leggings, handled their weapons. Each Marine carried more than one. In Billy's own hands rested a short .30 caliber carbine, and under his arm in a shoulder holster nestled a squat .45 automatic. He realized that with a flame thrower he had to get up close to the Japs, and suddenly he was no longer thinking of how he would do. For it was 0900, and the first tractors were scraping at the beach.

This was no ferrying movement, Billy saw. The amtracs came on in a violent, coordinated attack; they were heavily armored, and they fired machine guns and short 75mm howitzers at the beach. Employing speed, shock action and fire power, they gained all the momentum that the tactical mind of man and his engineering skill could devise.

Billy Farrel and the men around him were not aware of the acrid controversy between the high Marine and Naval commands over the duration of the softening bombardment. General Holland Smith, top-ranking Marine in the Central Pacific, had asked for eight days of neutralization; the Navy had refused more than three. There just didn't seem to be that much to shoot at on Iwo.

Refused his requested fires, Howlin' Mad Smith agreed with Major General Harry Schmidt, who would actually command the Fifth

Amphibious Corps ashore, that the assault should proceed on schedule and support fires be damned. They had not heard of Tadamichi Kuribayashi, and would not have cared if they had. There were more than 80,000 men in the Fifth Amphibious Corps, the largest Marine force ever sent in action, and they felt that Iwo could be quickly overrun, albeit with high casualties.

But even had they known of the controversy, Billy Farrel and the others would not have cared. They had their orders. Theirs was not to reason why — they had been given a job and they were Marines.

Also unknown to them as they reached the beaches was the fact that Lieutenant General Kuribayashi now made his first mistake. It was the only one he made but it would be fatal. He held back the order to fire, failing to realize the momentum of the assault. The Marines reached the beach and within minutes piled ashore a vast amount of men, vehicles and supplies — too much for them to be pushed off again.

Kuribayashi finally sprang his trap but now the enemy's jaws were about him as well. Marines and Japanese would be two scorpions in a bottle with no recourse but to sting each other to death in a fight to the finish.

The bulkheads of the armored amphibians clanged down, and Billy Farrel and the men about him plunged forward onto the sands of Iwo. Now it was individual Marine against the island and Billy soon found it was like pitting living flesh against reinforced concrete.

The first wave was on the beach and struggling to move inland, but behind them the following waves were catching hell. The air was dark with Jap mortar shells, and big guns from the base of Suribachi swept the beaches. Amtracs spouted fire, slewed and burned; many others sank. The assault lost momentum at once.

And up from the beach it was not much better. Marine Intelligence had erred badly. They had predicted firm sands, but the entire beach and island beyond was loose, coarse volcanic ash. Men sank in to their knees and the tracked vehicles bogged down, moving only with difficulty. The wheeled vehicles behind them sank and blocked the already crowded beaches.

And the four-foot slopes from the beaches, for which the Marines had been briefed, turned out to be fifteen feet. Armored vehicles could not cross the first ridge until bulldozers could come ashore and clear the way. But the lighter cargo tractors could cross the rise and they did — under a vicious, killing fire.

Now the Japs cut loose with everything they had, and the beaches became a hell of smoke, screaming fragments and confusion. A Company, like every other unit, began to come apart.

Whish-bram! Brram! Bram! Bram!

Billy Farrel knew the Japs were shooting the hell out of them, and they had to get inland. The men were being scattered as they sought whatever pitiful cover they could find on the beach. Already the platoon ammo carrier was lost as the Marines tried to crawl through the thick ash to the top of the first ridge.

Each step was a tremendous effort. Billy panted and, under the extra burden of the heavy Ronson, fell to his knees. He never would have made the first ridge except for the half-track that finally barrelled ahead of him, trying to bring its 75mm gun to bear. Billy caught onto the back of the armored vehicle, and it dragged him to the top of the ridge.

Fire blasted at him all along the ridge. He cursed because he had to get close with the flame thrower, and there were no Japs to be seen. Nor could be see any of his own men close by. The whole company had become scattered moving up from the beach.

But he could see mighty Suribachi rising more than five hundred feet to his left. The volcano loomed over him, blossoming flame and smoke. Awed, he stared at the smoke-wreathed mountain for a second, saw it blaze forth at the Marines, saw the flame from naval gunfire wash its slopes.

Ahead of him he could make out only a series of ridges like the one he had crossed. The whole island was a washboard of ash and rock, blazing fire. Now he could hear the wicked, ringing crack of small arms fire.

On the ridge he saw his first dead Marine, a crumpled figure in green lying face down on the pumice, blood running from beneath the man's combat pack. The corpse's legs were white in the morning sun, for he had discarded his leggings in the gritty ash.

The sight shook Billy Farrel. Then, after a few minutes, he wished he could see a Jap. Damn it, with the flame thrower he had to find one up close!

But he was now completely alone in a little corner of blasted volcanic sand, with shell fire splattering all about him. Back on the beaches he could hear the increased tempo of Jap fire — by noon it had reached a fantastic level. The southeast side of Iwo was dotted with dead and wounded Marines, and the runs from ship to shore had almost ceased. No boats could survive that constant lashing.

Billy Farrel found a shell hole and crawled into it. He didn't know where the rest of the company was, and he was not too disposed to crawl along the top of the ridge looking.

The hot, blazing, smoky afternoon passed and with the coming of night a chill wind blew in off the ocean, freezing him to the bone.

By dawn he was ready to move, come hell or high water. He crawled down the slopes to his right then encountered a young Marine runner who told him where the CP was. He headed for it immediately.

During the night more Marines had come ashore and now the beaches swarmed with armed men, backed by artillery. The push to gain more ground was starting up again. So far the Marines had only taken some three hundred yards of terrain inland from the water's edge.

Captain Wilkerson shouted at Billy, "There you are! We've been wondering where the flame throwers went — " He pointed up the ridge. "There's a Jap holed up behind that little clump there — "

The Jap fired then, pinning everybody down. A rifle squad opened up on him, driving him back to cover.

While the riflemen poured it on the Jap's hole, keeping him down, Billy crawled within range. He turned the nozzle of the Ronson, fired it, and sent a long stream of blazing jellied gasoline at the little hump of ground. He felt the heat blast back in his face.

The full stream hit the Jap. Burning at 3,000 degrees Fahrenheit, he didn't have time to scream — the shock killed him instantly. He slumped over in his hole and fried.

With the sniper out of the way, the company attempted to advance across the narrow neck of the island. But now it ran headlong into a defensive position, and the volume of small arms and mortar fire swelled. They rarely saw a Jap. When they located an enemy position, they put rifle fire on it, blasted it with the rocket launcher, got close and dropped a satchel charge into it. Then, if needed, Billy's flame thrower got its chance.

But when they finally crawled over the place from which fire had spat forth at them, they found no Japs. There were a few empty shell cases. That was all. They knew they were killing Japs but Kuribayashi's tactics robbed them of the satisfaction of seeing the enemy dead.

When pressed, the Japs popped down into their holes and withdrew through their deep tunnels. Sometimes they popped up again to the rear of the Marines, and the whole, heartbreaking operation had to be done again — in reverse.

The company finally came together under Captain Wilkerson's searching runners, but they only made one hundred yards that day.

They had seen only two Japs — the one Billy Farrel had fried and another who had been hit by pieces of burning white phosphorus from a 4.2 mortar burst. This unfortunate Japanese, his mustard-brown tunic smoldering, started up screaming from his covert, running wildly down the ridge. In open air nothing could stop phosphorus particles from burning. They burnt through heavy uniforms in a flash, seared deep into flesh.

But now the company was getting organized and they were learning how to fight the Jap defenders. The holes and bunkers could be reduced, provided the Marines went at it right.

Billy Farrel fell in with Andy Carter again, and Tony Stein with his Stinger. Stein had spent most of the first day carrying wounded men back to the beach, at all times through heavy fire.

A squad of riflemen under Sergeant Schultz from the 2nd Platoon supported Farrel and his boys. Together they began to comb the slopes and rocky ravines near the base of Suribachi for Japs.

Brrrrt — brrrt — bam!

A Nambu snarled at the advancing Marines and they hit the ground. Tony Stein opened up with his Stinger, spraying the sand and rock, his lips drawn back from his even teeth, his dark, good-looking face in a grimace. The Japanese fire slackened under the hail of slugs.

While Stein put a new belt in the Stinger, Schultz' men went to work with M-1s.

Crack! Crack!

Billy and his team were already in action. First, PFC Carter aimed his unwieldly bazooka at the tiny apertures from which the enemy fire blazed. He triggered the rocket launcher.

Whoosh — Bam!

Sand and soft rock spurted up, but the firing bunker was behind at least four feet of reinforced concrete. The small rocket charges could not penetrate.

Gaugeler, the man from Big Chi, risked his life to crawl on top of the sunken bunker and drop a satchel charge.

Brrrooom!

More smoke arose and the clouds of black pumice dust jarred loose made the Marines cough. But the Jap machine gun chattered again. The hole was too deep and strong to be reached by any ordinary weapon. It would take a bulldozer or a naval rifle shell to root the Japs out — or a flame thrower.

Sweating heavily, Tabert and Hardy edged closer with the second Ronson. Hardy had a limp cigarette, unlighted in his mouth, as he worked. He aimed the nozzle, pressed the firing release — but the flame thrower was ill-adjusted and the back blast caused the wet cigarette between his lips to burst into flame. Seared, Hardy leaped back.

The full stream, however, had reached the Jap bunker. The steel cover blazed red hot, and a thin stream of fiery spray shot through the apertures. There was a chorus of agonizing screams from deep in the earth.

Angrily Hardy sprayed the area again, his flame tongue reaching out in a mighty *whoosh*. Black, oily smoke drifted high, carrying an odor of cooked meat.

Even when the flame itself couldn't reach the lurking Japs, the flame thrower got them. The fierce flame burnt out all of the oxygen in their holes and quickly suffocated them. The flame thrower was a brutal, terrifying weapon but against an enemy who insisted on fighting below ground and who would never surrender, it was necessary.

In all wars it is you or the enemy, Billy thought, and if you waited too damn long to make up your mind who it was going to be, it was apt to be you. If it would save Marine lives, he'd fry all the Japs in the universe.

Foot by foot, yard by yard, leaving an irregular line of charred, stinking holes behind them, the Marines went across the narrow neck of the island.

That night Stein, Carter and Farrel huddled together in the same foxhole. As darkness fell, the Japs tried to infiltrate through the Marine positions, hoping to reach the installations on the beach. It was no haphazard push, no wild *banzai*, but a cool, murderous business.

All night the Marine lines blazed with grenade and rifle fire although no Japs came near Farrel's hole. They got one bad scare towards morning.

A scratching, slithering noise came toward their hole and all three of them immediately roused, their eyes and ears sharply attuned to danger.

"It's a Jap — "

"I see his eyes in the dark!"

"Shut up," Billy snapped and lifted his carbine. He could see the red gleam of the Jap's two eyes staring at him — but Jap eyes didn't shine in the dark.

"Oh, crap!" Tony Stein said explosively, dropping his heavy Stinger. The crawling thing paused at the side of their hole, mewing sadly. It was a small, bedraggled cat.

The next day A Company went across the narrow deck of Iwo and surrounded the base of Suribachi. And all day, while he was burning Japanese alive and Marines were being killed all around him, Billy Farrel felt sorry for that poor damned cat. The bleak volcanic rock was an inferno of gunfire and there was no water on Iwo . . .

The fourth day E Company drew the job of clearing Suribachi while Farrel's company rooted the Japs out of the numerous caves and ravines at its base. Some men from E made the crest and raised a small flag there on a piece of captured Jap pipe.

Three hours later someone in a policy-making position decided it would be better to fly a larger flag — one that could be seen over the entire island. The big flag was sent up, along with little Joe Rosenthal, an AP photographer.

The Marines staged a second flag-raising and Joe Rosenthal took a picture. A completely salty character who had taken hundreds of fine shots at the risk of his life, Joe later wondered which one his boss was raving about when he received radioed congratulations on his inspiring picture.

The rest of the 28th Marines, along with Billy Farrel, heard about the historic flag-raising later. At the moment they were too busy trying to clear a rough ravine at the base of the volcano. In one cave he blasted with his flame thrower the mop-up parties coming along behind the assault teams counted forty roasted Japs. With Schultz's men, he and Andy Carter cleared an entire ravine that afternoon. Towards night the first of the flame thrower tanks came up in support.

With Suribachi in Marine hands, Kuribayashi's eyes on the beach were blinded. Marine equipment was really beginning to come ashore and the obstacles blocking the beaches were cleared away.

With its heavy armor protection the tank could crank up to the very mouth of a cave or bunker, fire a tremendous jet of jellied gasoline for a longer range than the small portable throwers. With the tank along the work became almost routine.

Once Billy took time out to reflect that the Ronson people would probably be interested to know that all the Marines called the flame tanks Zippos.

It took a total of six more days to completely clear the slopes of Suribachi — and still the battle for Iwo was just beginning.

Eight days after the Marines crashed ashore on Iwo Jima, Radio Tokyo screamed boastfully that the American-held portion of the island was only "the size of the forehead of a cat."

Figuratively speaking the Jap claim was only too true.

The Marines had seventy thousand men ashore and hundreds of artillery pieces. Three full divisions, the 4th, 5th and 3rd, which had been in reserve, were in action on an area hardly bigger than the old south forty.

They had found the island one vast beachhead. There was never any cover, never any respite. Every foot of the island was honeycombed with Japs and all of them were fighting back — and they had plenty to fight with.

But General Kuribayashi's initial mistake would prove fatal in the end. The first Marine wave had washed ashore with such violence that it could never be washed off again. Now it was a war of attrition and, with superior forces, the Marines' eventual victory seemed assured. The only thing that was uncertain was how many Marines, if any, would live to see the final day.

But Tadamichi Kuribayashi was losing his thousands, too, and he had no reserves. A realist, Kuribayashi could see the handwriting on the wall. He could and would sell the lives of the Japanese dearly, but he could not win.

Some Japanese generals, living in a *samurai* dream world, would have sent glowing reports of victories to Tokyo. Grimly and honestly Kuribayashi asked for help.

From his deep bunker south of Kitano Point he radioed the homeland:

Send me ships and planes to attack the invading fleet; send me guns. Beyond all else, send me fresh troops to throw against the exhausted invaders. Send me these things and I will hold this island.

He must have wondered, where was the Imperial Navy? The Imperial Air Force?

The Imperial Air Force tried to ease the situation for the Jap defenders. It flew large sorties against the fleet surrounding Iwo. But between the homeland and Iwo lay a powerful American carrier force, with skilled night fighters. The carrier force, however, suffered severe blows. The *Bismarck Sea* went to the bottom and the *Saratoga* was badly mauled. But only two weak flights of Japanese planes reached Iwo.

As for the Imperial Navy, unknown to most Army commanders, it was already rusting on the bottom of the ocean.

Had Kuribayashi had such support, Iwo Jima would probably have become an American disaster.

Without these things, I cannot hold, he radioed, finally.

He got no help. There was none to give him.

Then Tadamichi Kuribayashi knew he was going to die. But not for him the ceremonial knife of General Saito or the suicidal *banzai* charge. Nor would he surrender — although Generals Cates and Erskine, who had come to respect the little potbellied man with the hard head, sent personal messages promising fair treatment. General Kuribayashi prepared to die, and his preparation was to kill and maim as many Marines as possible before the end.

With his stubborn, brilliantly-executed defense he would wound or kill one Marine for each man he commanded on Volcano Island.

The United States Marines will be quite happy if they never encounter another Tadamichi Kuribayashi though their history extends a thousand years.

From the blasted slopes of Suribachi Billy Farrel's men could see the black pall of smoke hanging over the central part of Iwo; they could hear the incessant gunfire night and day, and they knew the battle was going badly. The rest of their 5th Division was in trouble, and the 4th was exhausted. The 3rd, originally in reserve, had come into the battle and was being bled white rapidly.

To the 28th Marines came orders to move north. As Lieutenant Colonel Charles Shepard put it, their orders were to 1) *secure this lousy piece of real estate so we can get the hell off it,* 2) *help as many Nips as possible fulfill their oath to die for the Emperor.*

They did both, but the doing took twenty-six more days.

A Company moved in single file across a blasted land where the flotsam of battle and the stench of death lay all about. Noxious fumes spewed upward from fissures in the earth, and men slipped and stumbled in the loose ash, hurting themselves on volcanic rock.

As they moved north, the loose ash of the south gave way to a soft, andesitic lava. The terrain became incredibly rough and broken, split by fissures and ravines, from many of which vile steam spouted into the air. The ghastly, sweetish scent of unburied dead clung to their nostrils.

Billy Farrel figured it was enough to gag a maggot. This section of Iwo seemed a corner of a weird planet in outer space.

Moving slowly toward the sound of fighting, they crossed a devastated air field, and skirted the mouth of a vast sulfur mine. The ground grew rougher and they went more slowly yet.

Here, in the northern section of the island, they met the Japanese last main defense.

The sudden rain of small arms and mortar fire that buffeted the company was unbelievable. The advance stopped and the company melted away behind rocks and into holes in the lava. Captain Wilkerson, the skipper, moved ahead to peer over a small rise in the lava floor.

Spang!

Wilkerson rolled back down the incline, shot between the eyes.

Spang! Spang!

Rifle fire from hidden Jap snipers lashed at the company. Billy Farrel cursed, trying to see where the shots came from. The smokeless powder the Japs used beat anything he'd ever seen — there was not even a wisp of smoke to betray the firing apertures.

Crack! Wow-wow-wow!

Wiry Sergeant Schultz fell dead, bright blood staining his dark, sweaty beard. Private Siorotiak gasped, shot through both buttocks.

Tony Stein, whose Stinger had been shot out of his hand near Suribachi, was impatient at being pinned down. He moved to his left, seeking higher ground.

Spang!

Stein fell, his handsome, dark features relaxing in death. He never learned that he had been recommended for the Medal of Honor for his feats with the wounded on D Day, or that the medal would be awarded posthumously.

Billy had heard the old talk back in Hawaii, how the Japs couldn't hit the side of a barn with a rifle. Once, they told him, a colonel on Guadalcanal walked up and down the battle line in shorts, carrying only a stick to prove this to his men.

But this wasn't the 'Canal and to expose yourself even for an instant meant death.

Captain Parsons, who had just been promoted but who had stayed with the company as exec, took command. Doubling as a demolition man, he was hit and lost a leg.

Grimly the company fought back and Billy Farrel's depleted little team went into action. Inch by inch they tried to clear away the Japs firing from each rise in the ground. Before night fell both Gaugeler and Talbert were killed by a mortar round. The same burst wounded two more Marines. Billy's assault team was now almost gone.

When darkness covered the battle-scarred land, the company stopped. They were in the middle of a lot of Japanese. They could have pulled back to safer ground, but that would be giving up soil for which their buddies had died. They didn't even discuss pulling back.

They built a crude foxhole in the lava beds, together, and figured they'd hold it. Billy and Andy Carter were foxhole buddies and that was the best kind there was.

Billy had discarded his empty flame thrower a long time back. Now he carried a carbine. The tall, slim Carter — the laconic youth from Paducah, Kentucky — carried his own M-1 plus a long Arisaka rifle, complete with bayonet, which he had latched onto while moving north. He called it his souvenir.

After dark, in spite of frequent flares, the Japs began to crawl from their holes and bunkers. They made noise on the lava, moving into the Marine lines.

The Marines had no real line of battle — they were scattered in a series of holes over a large stretch of hellish terrain. In the night's gloom each tiny position was on its own. No one could see to fire in support of another hole.

Billy and Andy Carter had only a few grenades, which was the most effective weapon in the night.

They heard crawlers approach them and they threw grenades at the noises. *Blam!* Rock showered down on them and for a little while the noises ceased.

Later they heard noises behind them and threw two more grenades. They were not about to leave the hole to see if they had killed any Japs. After it grew quiet, Andy suggested that Billy get some sleep, while he took the first watch.

When a man is tired enough, he can sleep on naked rock. Billy sprawled out on the deck, making a pillow out of his steel helmet.

The rapid, ringing crash of an M-1 brought Billy Farrel to his feet. Carter had emptied a clip into the night in front of the foxhole. He grabbed his own carbine, knelt down beside Carter. They didn't speak.

Pop!

A flare went off overhead, hurling eerie, flickering yellowish light across the torn landscape. Just in front of the foxhole Billy counted four sprawled Japanese, brought down by Carter's quick work with the M-1.

The flare fizzled out and a voice screeched in Japanese from down the ridge. There were scrapings on the rock, coming closer.

"Throw a grenade!" Billy said.

"We're out."

Carter took aim with his still warm rifle. It would not fire; the piece was fouled. The volcanic soil and pumice-stone played havoc with gas-operated rifles, jamming their bolts after a few rounds. Carter threw the rifle away. They had only a carbine between them now.

"Hang on," Carter said. "There are some more rifles at the CP. I'll go down and get me one."

Billy nodded and Carter straddled the lava wall and crawled off in the dark. Billy didn't envy him one bit. He thought he saw something off to the right and snapped his carbine to his shoulder. To his horror he found the bolt wouldn't close. The carbine, also, was useless.

A small, black grenade bounced out of the night and came to rest at his feet. Before he could move, it exploded with a blinding flash. In a red haze, seeing only brilliant flashes before his eyes, Billy fell back against the side of the foxhole. He was almost totally deaf.

He tried to move and discovered his left leg was broken. He also found that his left hand was hanging to his wrist by a shred. Oddly, he felt no pain then — none at all.

He drifted into a sort of shock then, until he heard Andy crawling back up the slope. Andy straddled the rock again, but there was no time for conversation.

"*Look out!*"

Two big Japs ran out of the night, heading straight for Andy. He pulled the trigger of his new M-1; one of the Japs was blown down at pointblank range, but the second ran at Andy, slashing with a glittering *samurai* saber.

Andy put the muzzle on him, too, but the M-1 had jammed. The saber whirled and fell. Andy threw up his hands, took the cut against his left arm. Blood spurted across the foxhole. The big Jap screamed curses, tried to strike again. But Andy Carter, his left hand almost ruined, had scooped up the captured Jap rifle and held it in front of him awkwardly. The Jap impaled himself on its long, sharp bayonet, shrieked shrilly and died.

Andy Carter was dripping blood all over the place as he tried to help Billy. "Go on back to the CP," Billy told him.

Because of the broken leg Billy couldn't move without help — more help than the bleeding, dizzy Carter could give him.

"I'll go back and get another rifle," Carter muttered. He struggled out of the foxhole and crawled away.

Head slowly clearing, Billy lay in the hole, wondering if Andy would make it to the CP. He didn't think Andy would get back — he was hurt too bad. His leg and shattered hand didn't hurt too much, but there was a small wound in his right armpit — just where he could scratch with his good hand — that was driving him crazy.

A few minutes later he heard someone coming up to the foxhole. Two men climbed over the rim of lava and squatted down in front of him.

They were Japs.

They only looked at Billy once. With blood all over him, both his own and Andy's, they figured him for dead. It was a serious mistake — the last one they ever made.

Without shifting, Billy could just reach the .45 in his shoulder. He hoped to God there was a round in the chamber, but he couldn't remember. He eased the big pistol out slowly, suddenly cocked it, and jammed it against a Jap. The enemy soldier was blown over backward as the gun blasted; his tunic flamed briefly from powder burns.

The second Jap was too startled to use his rifle. He reached for a small grenade, tapped it against his helmet — the Jap method of arming their grenades. Then he dropped the grenade in the hole and leaped out of it.

Desperately Billy scrabbled for the grenade. He got the pistol under it, scooped it up into the air. Suddenly it exploded, shredding his pistol hand in one violent flash. But it also killed the Jap standing outside the hole.

Fainting, Billy sank back against the side of the hole. If any more Japs came he was finished.

Maybe he was finished, anyway — both of his hands were gone and he was bleeding freely.

It could not have been many minutes before a naval corpsman arrived at the hole. It was Sam Drinkwater, hospital corpsman from San Antonio. Carter had made it to the CP and he had been evacuated to the rear, for he had lost too much blood already. But he had not gone until Drinkwater promised to go up to help Billy Farrel.

Drinkwater looked Billy over carefully. "Shoot, you'll make it," he said cheerfully. "One of these days you and me'll see each other in San Antone — "

Painfully then, he lifted Billy over the foxhole rim and dragged him down toward the CP. About halfway down they met another corpsman moving toward them. One thing about the corpsmen — if they heard there was a hurt Marine around, they went to get him.

"Give me some sulfa," Drinkwater told the new corpsman. "I'm almost out and Farrel needs some bad."

"I don't have much left," the second corpsman argued.

"Goddamnit, I don't care whose sulfa you use — just get some on me!" Billy croaked, listening to them squabble.

That got some action, finally.

They took Billy Farrel back down to the beach, most of the way under fire. Then they got him out to the hospital ship and back to the States. Meanwhile back on Iwo the struggle went on. There were going to be a lot of Billy Farrels before it ended.

But he made it. And they gave Andy Carter the Navy Cross for what he did, and as Billy was to say later, they gave him something, too.

Maybe it was because they had a certain quota they had to give out, he said, but anyway, they presented him with the Medal of Honor on the White House lawn.

And Sam Drinkwater was a better prophet than he knew. One year later, to the very day, Drinkwater and Farrel, who was with the Veteran's Administration and learning to use his new steel hands quite well, had coffee together on Houston Street three blocks up from the Alamo.

Iwo Jima fell. Shuddering from their losses, the United States Marines turned to the next island on their time table.

Just south of the home islands of Japan lay the Ryukyus, last stop before the scheduled invasion of the homeland itself. With both Okinawa, largest of the Ryukyus, and Luzon in American hands, the projected assault on the Empire of Japan would be ready for staging. . . .

Because Okinawa was a large land mass compared to the type of islands the Marines had been assaulting, Okinawa would be primarily an Army show under Army top command. Sustained warfare on land, after all, was the function of the Army. Two Marine Divisions were made part of the Tenth Army under General Simon Bolivar Buckner, for it was expected that the beaches of Okinawa would be hot, and crossing defended beaches was the Marines' stock in trade.

No one expected the landings on Okinawa to be easy. The memory of Iwo Jima was very green, for on that reeking bit of hell the guns had just ceased firing. The closer the Marines came to the homeland of Japan, the rougher the going they encountered.

Okinawa was the last island of the war. Soon after its fall, stunned by the atomic bomb, Japan would surrender. It had already long since been defeated, step by step, island by island, across the broad Pacific. From islands secured by the blood and bones of countless Marines, sailors and soldiers, long-range bombers had turned the home isles into a shambles.

Okinawa was the last island — and what the Japanese did there would be the highest and most sincere tribute to the Marine's skill at amphibious warfare. The Japs would choose not to fight on the beaches.

It was the last island of the war — and the last island for thousands of American fighting men, who would never leave it.

Ten

The Last Island: Okinawa 1945

"We must make it our basic principle to allow the enemy to land in full. Until he penetrates our positions and loses freedom of movement inside our most effective system of fire power. . . . we must patiently and prudently hold our fire. Then we shall open fire and wipe out the enemy." Battle Instruction Number 8, issued March 8, 1945, by Lieutenant General Mitsuru Ushijima, Commanding Ryukyu Gunto, Okinawa.

They breakfasted on oranges, steak and eggs, coffee cake and ice cream, and when they fed you that way in this war, Corporal Cherry Reed knew, they were getting you ready for the kill.

Afterward the men of the 4th Marine Division went topside to watch the preliminary bombardment of the beaches west of Yontan Airfield in the middle portion of Okinawa.

There were more than a thousand ships in the flotilla, the largest number of warships ever seen, and they did not make the mistake of Iwo — the bombardment was long and it was complete. Ten old battleships, numerous cruisers and destroyers, and dozens of rocket and mortar ships rocked the beaches hour after hour.

Then the amtracs were loaded with men of the 4th and 22nd Marines and they headed for the shore. It was an hour past dawn, April 1, 1945.

To a lot of the Marines it was April Fool's Day and they guessed the joke was on them. But to Corporal Cherry Reed, Fire Team Leader, 3rd Squad, 1st Platoon of F Company, 4th Marines, it was Easter Sunday. His widowed mother had seen that Cherry Reed had a good, religious upbringing.

He was twenty years old, with curly brown hair, hazel eyes and a snub-nosed face that would stay youthful over the years, but he was no kid. Cherry Reed, like most of the men around him this morning, had been two years in the Pacific and had seen action on Emirau, Bougainville, and Guam. Most of Captain Holmgreen's company had come from the old Raider Battalions when those outfits had been broken up. ,

They had told Cherry and his men to expect a hot beach and he expected it going in. But he had seen hot beaches before, and he was more worried about drowning in the surf than being hit by the Japanese.

On Guam his amtrac had struck a coral reef and tipped over. Cherry's BAR man had drowned trying to fight his way ashore.

And they had touted the Marines on the liver flukes that supposedly infested Okinawa. The liver flukes lurked in the lakes and streams, and if you waded in or drank the water, you got them. Inside you they made for the liver and once they reached it, you'd had it.

Jap gunfire seemed a lot cleaner.

Cherry Reed came in with the sixth wave. Usually that was one of the attack formations that caught it. In his plunging amtrac, squatting down with his squad leader, Rex Guyman from Utah, and his buddy, Bob McCurry of Tennessee, Cherry was shivering now, but it was not because of Japs or even liver flukes.

To men just up from the training areas on Guadalcanal, Okinawa was cold as a witch's you know what.

The sixth wave met no coral reefs and it floated all the way up to the firm beach — the first time such a thing had happened in the Pacific. The 1st Platoon plunged from the amtrac, spreading out, but there was no fire. There was nothing at all except a clear, blue sky, a cool wind and a beach full of Marines.

We could hold Easter services on the beach, Cherry Reed thought. *And they told us this would be the toughest one of all —*

Plunging ahead, past the scrub trees fringing the ocean and past the massive, ornate Okinawan tombs scattered over the countryside, he began to wonder if there were such things as liver flukes. Intelligence — even Marine Intelligence — was not always perfect.

But there was no time to muse over the strangeness of it all. Colonel Shapley had been surprised, too, but he ordered the regiment to advance. Almost running, the 4th Marines went through sugar cane fields, flanked by woods apparently of pine or cedar, and sped along the crests of small hills. The countryside was beautiful and the air was crisp. To the north the terrain appeared wilder and more mountainous.

They passed a series of caves and proceeded cautiously. They had had experience with Nip caves before. But they met no fire and, amazingly, even found Nip ammunition stockpiled in some of the caves. But the Nips themselves were nowhere in sight.

They met Okinawans — small, brown, frightened people who could only bob heads and try to smile at these frightening, fair-skinned giants clad in green dungarees and carrying large and potent weapons.

Beside Cherry, Clyde Workman, a short, stocky, cotton-headed Californian, kept shouting "Okinawa — Okinawa!" at the natives. They seemed to understand that, and kept nodding and bowing, but you could hardly say that communication had been established. At any rate the natives, themselves conquered by the Japanese long before, gave no trouble.

In an hour the 4th Marines reached Yontan Airfield. Their mission was to secure it and they had expected to reach it by L plus 3. The airfield seemed deserted.

Around the landing strips Cherry saw long bamboo poles emplaced to resemble AA guns, and some cleverly-rigged dummy aircraft. But no Nips were about.

They secured the field and by late afternoon they were on the line they had expected to reach on Love Plus Five. They were almost a week ahead of schedule.

Up at Regiment and Division, Cherry knew, a lot of plans were being scrapped. But he knew what the outcome would be. When in doubt, the Marines would advance.

They were preparing the evening meal when a Nip plane roared over the field and banked. Everyone hit the dirt or crawled into the brush. But the plane did not fire. It circled the field, went out to sea, then sputtered in for a smooth landing while the Marines watched open-jawed.

The small Nip pilot cut the engine, shrugged out of his parachute pack, and hopped out of the plane. Then he saw the Marines coming out of cover. His narrow eyes widened in amazement.

He made a fatal mistake — he reached for his pistol. Cherry, Workman, McCurry and a dozen others opened fire with their rifles. The Nip airman was slammed back, dead, and the plane behind him was riddled with bullets.

Bob McCurry drawled, "I guess they got ten per cent on their side, too, who don't get the word — "

That night there was a scattering of shots on the perimeter, nothing more. At 0715 next morning the advance continued. That day, as the 4th and 22nd Marines spread fan-like over the green rice paddies cut by steep slopes and scrubby pine trees, there were several brief, bitter small unit actions. Love Company was ambushed in a ravine and chopped to pieces, finally breaking through and killing 150 Nips. 1st Battalion hit strong resistance and mopped up some 250 enemy troops by late afternoon.

But this was scattered, sporadic resistance. There was no Nip defensive line, and neither the 4th nor 22nd Marines, with the 29th Regiment in reserve, were slowed down. The rapid, almost running advance continued.

F Company, like all the Marines, outran its supply trains. No one had planned for the war to go like this, and reefs across the landing beaches delayed the unloading of supplies more than had been contemplated. By L plus 2, Cherry Reed and his men were making do on half a canteen of water per day and very little food.

They weren't shot at too much, but they were starving to death, passing among green fields and lovely, vegetable-laden gardens; they were licking lips cracked with thirst while they waded across clear, swift mountain streams.

It was Van Camp who changed the last. The tall, skinny Jerseyite crossed a stream, and was carefully wringing out his socks, for they had been told the liver flukes could enter the bare skin itself. At the age of fourteen Van Camp had run away from home, and he had run away from a few reform schools on the route, too. The day he landed on Okinawa he was a veteran of several courts-martial, and he was sweating out six months' probation on a Bad Conduct Discharge.

The trouble with Van Camp was simple. He was that rare breed who could fight superbly, but could not be a parade ground Marine. On the 'Canal Van Camp stole a jeep, broke into the officers' winery and had himself a party. Worse, he was discovered asleep on guard duty, for Van Camp knew there weren't any Japs left on Guadalcanal to guard against.

He had been in the old 2nd Raider Battalion with Cherry Reed and, strangely, the two were close friends. Now, feeling the cool water drip from his fingers on Okinawa while his canteen was dry, Van Camp said, "To hell with the liver flukes!" He dipped the empty canteen in clear water and took a long swig.

In two minutes everybody was drinking, and that was the last Cherry Reed heard of liver flukes.

In five days the 6th Division reached its L plus 15 positions. Now their orders were to press on and secure all of northern Okinawa while the Tenth Army pressed south.

The 4th Marines went across the Ishikawa Isthmus onto the Motobu Peninsula, which was steep and almost impassable country. The natives, a tough race of mountain farmers, laid out their poor fields on seemingly impossible terraces. The mountainous ground was superb for defense, had it been strongly defended.

Here on Mount Yaetake the regiment met the Nipponese 44th Mixed Brigade under a Colonel Udo. Udo fought well, but he was outnumbered and outgunned. While Cherry Reed's battalion supported, the rest of the 4th and the 29th Marines took Yaetake and wiped out Udo and his brigade.

From then on it was a mopping-up operation in northern Okinawa. At the end of the month, on May 2, the 27th Division, US Army, relieved the 6th Division. Three quarters of the island now was in American hands and the Marines had suffered less than 1,500 casualties.

Meanwhile, in the south, the Army's XXIV Corps had found the Japanese.

High in Shuri Castle, the old seat of the Okinawan kings, Lieutenant General Mitsuru Ushijima and his Chief of Staff, General Cho, understood two things well — there was no stopping the terrible American naval gunfire and armored amphibious assaults on the beaches of Okinawa, and the average Japanese soldier's instinct was to live, fight and die underground.

Because the High Command had feared the blow might fall on Formosa, the Ryukyu Command had been stripped of a division. General Ushijima realized he could not defend the entire coastline of an island seventy miles in length with only 79,000 soldiers and some 10,000 naval personnel.

His plans did not include a defense of the beaches. They did include a withdrawal southward to a natural line of defense just north of Naha, the modern capital. Here, across the entire island from Yonabaru on the east to Naha in the west, rose a series of coral hills honeycombed with caves.

Stiff-backed, the stocky, short Ushijima gave orders. Along this line every hill was made a fortress, tunneled, hollowed-out, and scarred with multiple, octopus-type firing pits.

He had many units, *shitai* and *butai*, heavy in artillery. Ushijima buried these in the earth. The larger guns were put on rails so that they could be run up to apertures, fired, and withdrawn to safety during bombardments.

At the center of the line rose the towering Shuri hill mass and the fortress of Shuri itself, lair of the ancient pirate kings of Okinawa. Once the lords of Shuri had paid tribute to the Chinese Emperor. Now Ushijima, representative of a different emperor, planned to exact tribute from the *Amerikajin* — in blood. This line he would hold while a wind from the north would wipe out the barbarian invader.

In the time of Kublai Khan a hundred thousand Mongol and Chinese invaders had descended on the coast of Japan. While the *samurai* in lacquered armor had held the fierce Mongol bowmen at bay on the beaches the *kamikaze* — divine wind — had sprung up, destroying the ships of the invaders. The Mongol assault had ended in total failure and the homeland had been saved.

Now Ushijima felt that his modern *samurai* — those who serve — would hold the invader at bay before Shuri while a new and modern divine wind howled down from the home isles to complete their destruction.

The *kamikaze* played a vital part in Ushijima's planning. Planes, piloted by fanatics who had already celebrated their own funerals, would crash-dive the American fleet. The attack on Okinawa would be driven back with terrible loss.

If the *kamikaze* failed, Ushijima and his warriors were doomed. But no one expected such a fearsome weapon to fail. Even the Americans had an inkling of what was coming and were nervous.

In actuality, the fleet off Okinawa would live through days of hell. Picket boats would be sunk, sailors killed — but not one major warship would be lost. The *kamikaze* was unsound from the start. Like most Japanese tactics it could annoy, even terrify, but it could not win.

To ensure the safety of mighty Shuri's flank, Ushijima and Cho agreed it would be necesary to hold three small hills forming an arrowhead pointed north. These low hills, masses of volcanic rock and coral, were fortified to the utmost. They were the key to the whole Naha-Yonabaru Line, and to the island. If they were lost, Shuri could be flanked, Naha taken, and the days of Ushijima and his *samurai* would be numbered.

The foremost hill resembled a rectangular sugar loaf, those behind it a half moon and a horseshoe. On them the campaign would be won or lost.

The Tenth Army's advance plunged south against the Shuri Line — and halted. The easy days on Okinawa were over. The 6th Marine Division was recalled from the north. In the first days of May they marched south through heavy rains. They went into action along the Asa Kawa River, and by May 12th had advanced 2,000 yards. The 22nd Marines, bearing the brunt of the assault, lost more than eight hundred men.

Just before G Company, 22nd Marines, rose three rather insignificant coral hills. Captain Stebbins had no reason to suspect they were any different from any of the hills G Company had been crossing and clearing. It was slow, heartbreaking work, using what Army General Buckner called the "blowtorch and corkscrew method" — rooting out the dug-in Japs with flame throwers and demolitions, but slowly, surely, the Marines were moving southward.

Captain Owen Stebbins organized a tank-infantry attack on the first of the hills which he called Sugar Loaf. He was completely unaware that he was touching Mitsuru Ushijima's sorest nerve.

It was more than a thousand yards of open ground from the nearest cover to the slopes of Sugar Loaf. G Company advanced rapidly, the supporting tanks grinding along beside them. For the first hundred yards there was only light, scattered fire. Then without warning, all three hills ahead blazed fire. On each, guns had been sighted to fire in mutual suport, and from the high hill mass of Shuri itself Japanese cannon could range the entire area.

Blam! Blam! Blam!

The two lead platoons of G Company were pinned down under a hail of steel.

The tanks drew vicious 47mm AT fire and were forced to halt.

Captain Stebbins was following the lead platoons with Lt. Dale Bair and forty men of the 3rd Platoon. He shouted, "Let's go — let's go!"

Marines had been pinned down by fire before, and a vigorous attack had carried the day. 3rd Platoon hit a solid wall of fire and steel. Owen Stebbins' legs were riddled by machine gun bullets; he fell, a stretcher case. Dale Bair, six-feet-two and 225 pounds, was an easy man to see and follow. He took command and continued to lead the advance up Sugar Loaf.

At, the end of a hundred yards Bair had only twelve men left on their feet. His own left arm dangled uselessly. But Bair's courage matched his bulk. Grimacing with pain, he cradled a machine gun in his good right arm and bellowed at some of the pinned-down Marines to come on. A dozen of them joined his own small force. Under Bair's urging, the tanks took up their advance once more.

Bair reached the top of Sugar Loaf. Four of his original platoon reached it with him. Behind them the slope was littered with dead and injured Marines.

Now the Jap defense went wild. A frantic rain of small arms, mortar, and heavy artillery fire beat against Sugar Loaf. The tankers threw out smoke grenades to try to screen their vehicles, and dismounted to help the wounded climb on the tanks. The few surviving Marines crouched behind the tanks, trying to see something to fire at.

Bair stood on the skyline, a perfect target, firing his light machine gun against the caves and rifle pits blazing at him. Seeing him, the Marines about him fought on — it was impossible to be afraid with his stalwart example to inspire and encourage them.

But in a few minutes Bair had no unhurt men left. Reluctantly he retreated down the hill, taking his wounded with him.

He called for supporting fires to be put on the hill — but the enemy positions were invulnerable to air strikes, naval gunfire and tanks. They could only be reduced at close range, by riflemen and demolition squads.

Three times more that memorable afternoon Dale Bair tried to take Sugar Loaf and three times he failed. When night came, Sugar Loaf still loomed before the Marines, seemingly invulnerable.

Now began a six day battle which would rank in Marine annals with Tenaru, Bloody Nose Ridge and Suribachi.

Many times Marines stood on Sugar Loaf, but they could not stay. Again and again they took the hill only to be driven back. The story of Major Courtney and his handful of Marines is typical of the whole, bloody six days:

Late in the afternoon of May 14th, 2nd Battalion, 22nd Marines, attacked Sugar Loaf with Companies F and G abreast, supported by tanks and screened by smoke.

After two hours of fighting, only 40 men and one tank remained of the entire attack force. They had reached the front slope of Sugar Loaf, and there they had been shattered. Daylight was fading, and with it the heart of the 2nd Battalion. They were almost out of ammunition and the survivors were dispirited.

Major Henry A. Courtney, Jr., the battalion exec, had been with the assault companies all day. A keen-eyed, courageous, quiet man, he was considered one of the division's top officers.

Now, with daylight dying, he saw a small party of ammo handlers working their way across the blasted wastes toward the survivors on the reeking slope of Sugar Loaf. Battalion was trying to help the embattled companies; the party carried a few rations and a great quantity of grenades and ammunition.

These ammo bearers were an odd lot, runners, field musics, cooks — not riflemen. But Courtney stopped them in the dusk, and during one of those weird, unearthly quiets which sometimes fall over a battle field, he said, "Men, we've got to take the top of this hill tonight. If we don't, the Japs will come down here to drive all of us away again in the morning."

The ammo carriers looked at him.

"I have a plan. If it works, we'll take the top of the hill. I want volunteers — for a *banzai* of our own!"

Nobody said anything. They all knew what it was like on the crest of Sugar Loaf. Courtney, his face dirty, tired and drawn, continued, "Some of us are never going to come down again, but that hill's got to be taken. We're going to do it. Well, what do you say?"

All twenty-six of the carriers volunteered.

Twenty more men from the shattered companies along the base of the hill wanted to go, too. That gave Courtney forty-six men — a good platoon.

Eyes gleaming, Courtney explained his simple plan. They would attack under the cover of darkness, in line formation. When they reached the top, they would throw a terrific barrage of grenades to keep the Japs off while they dug in on the crest.

When he was sure everyone had the word, Courtney called for mortar fire on Sugar Loaf. Then he said, "I'm going to the top. Who's coming along?"

They raced up the slope quickly, unseen by the enemy. On the crest some of them hurled grenades furiously while others tried to dig holes. Alerted, the Japs threw rifle and machine gun fire at them; from the caves and bunkers on the supporting Half Moon and Horseshoe a hail of bullets hammered at them. The Japs on Sugar Loaf's reverse slopes tossed back grenades of their own.

But the Marines dug in and, as midnight came, they were holding on. Then they heard noises on the back slope of the hill. It sounded like many Japs were gathering in the dark. Major Courtney listened intently.

"Men, I think they're going to *banzai* us — "

The men around him were ready. Corporal Rusty Golar readied his light .30 machine gun; Private Don Kelly gripped his M-1. Golar was a brawny redhead who had developed his giant muscles on the San Francisco waterfront. On Guam he had won a Bronze Star for heroism. Back on the 'Canal he had told the other Marines, "Look, I'm one of these glory-hunters. I'm out for glory and I'm out for Japs!"

On Sugar Loaf Corporal Rusty Golar found both.

Henry Courtney realized that within seconds a horrifying wave of screeching Japanese would sweep over the top of Sugar Loaf — and he had far less than forty-six men now. In the dark, with the Marines scattered, the *banzai* charge would cut them to pieces.

Courtney stood up. "Let's give 'em our own *banzai!*"

His voice rose, reached them all as they lay huddled about the hill.

"Grab all the grenades you can carry. We'll charge over the crest and let 'em have it!"

Teeth gleaming in his dust-stained, stubbled face, Henry Courtney led the charge. A flight of grenades whistled down at the startled Japs.

Blam! Blam!

Taken by surprise, the Japs fled back into their caves. But Courtney was on top of them.

"Keep coming, men! There's a mess of them down here!"

The night flared redly with exploding grenades and the orange-purple flashes of rifles and machine guns. Men screamed and shouted. But Courtney got too far ahead of his own men. A grenade bounced out of the night from a hidden cave.

Brram!

Henry Courtney was thrown to the slanting ground, streaming blood.

The Jap threat, however, had melted away. On the crest of Sugar Loaf it was almost quiet.

A cold wind blew up out of the East China Sea, bringing rain and misery to the huddled survivors on the hill. In the rain and bitter chill Major Henry Courtney bled his life away.

Morning approached and his little group, hardly more than a dozen now, still held onto the crest of Sugar Loaf. Gradually the dawn came, shrouded in mist. And out of the gray clouds the Japs swarmed, buzzing and angry.

Corporal Golar had placed his light machine gun up forward where it had the best field of fire — but where it was also exposed to the Japs on Horseshoe.

As the Japs closed, Golar sent streams of tracer ripping into the hillsides around him, holding them at bay. Immediately, he drew fire from the adjoining hill. Bullets tore at the earth around him.

Golar realized he was being fired on from the flank. "Yeah!" he said. He whirled the machine gun around. Helmeted head bobbing up and down while he crouched on one knee, he poured fire into Horseshoe. And he drove the Jap gunners to cover.

"Yeah — yeah!" he bellowed, swinging back to fire at a closer target. A few yards from his position, Private Don Kelly tried to give him cover with an M-1.

Most of the other men on Sugar Loaf were dead or wounded and out of the fight. Ammo was low — during the night no ammo bearer had been able to make it up the hill. With daylight resupply was impossible.

Soon Golar's .30 ran dry. He yelled across to Kelly, "Gotta use what I got left."

He pulled out his .45 automatic, emptied it at the Japs. When it clicked empty, he hurled it across the hill and into a cave. Weaponless, Golar pawed at the earth around the fallen Marines, looking for grenades.

He found two, pulled the pins, and threw them down the hill. *Blam! Blam!*

With the few seconds of time the grenades bought, Rusty Golar found a BAR in the hands of a dead Marine. He whirled about, the BAR at his hip. He was back in business.

Thump-thump-thump! The infiltrating Japs leaped for cover.

Suddenly the automatic rifle jammed. Cursing, Golar heaved it down the hill.

"Nothing more to give 'em now," he boomed to Kelly. "Let's get some of these wounded guys down the hill!"

Walking through a crescendo of enemy fire, Golar bent over a Marine shot through the chest. "Have you back in sick bay in no time," he murmured.

He lifted the seriously hurt man easily in his powerful arms and started down the hill to safety.

Spang!

Kelly saw Rusty Golar stagger, his feet dragging. He bent over, laying the wounded man down gently on the ground. He looked back toward Kelly's anxious face, surprise in his eyes. He took a couple of steps and suddenly sat down.

Golar reached up to his helmet, pushed it forward over his face as if he were going to sleep. When Kelly reached him, he was dead.

Kelly and fourteen live Marines made it back down the hill under terrific fire.

It turned out that Major Courtney had been correct about what would happen unless the top of Sugar Loaf were held. The Japs counterattacked strongly, driving the 22nd Marines completely away from the hill.

For three more days the see-saw battle raged across the blasted coral ridges. Finally, the 29th Marine Regiment was able to flank Sugar Loaf, surround it, and put men on Horseshoe.

But after dark on the 18th, the enemy reinforced and attacked, firing white phosphorus shells into the weak Marine units holding Horseshoe. They retreated and Japs began to infiltrate back onto Sugar Loaf.

Both the 29th Marines and the 22nd Regiment were exhausted and cut to pieces. They had almost captured the vital terrain, but a last strong push was needed.

On May 19, the 4th Marines entered the fight.

Cherry Reed's squad spent the night of the 18th back from Sugar Loaf, dug-in wet, hilly farmland. The smell was terrible, for the Okinawans, like most Orientals, used human fertilizer extensively. The whole country smelled like a head after a beer party.

And the 4th Marines were shelled heavily by the big Jap, guns on Shuri. The Japs realized their whole line was now in danger and they were throwing in everything they had.

Soon after daylight 2nd Battalion of the 4th moved out. There were still Japs on Sugar Loaf, but their mission was to cut between Sugar Loaf and Half Moon to seize Horseshoe.

Under vicious, incessant shelling, they shoved off to do the job. In the open country the companies scattered, spreading out to lessen the targets available to the gunners on Shuri. Somehow, the 1st Platoon of F Company got separated from the rest, but it didn't matter too much. They knew what the mission was.

They passed between Sugar Loaf and Half Moon, drawing fire, and paused at the slopes of Horseshoe. Here Lt. McNeil set the 2nd squad up as a base of fire, to pound the hill. He himself attacked up the front slope with the 1st squad, under the 2nd's covering fire.

The 3rd squad he ordered to flank completely around the hill, to strike it in the rear.

There were thirteen men in Rex Guyman's squad, counting Corporal Cherry Reed. Most of them were old hands. They cut around the hill, found a narrow gauge railroad and continued down the tracks for nearly a mile. Their maps showed that the railway cut in behind Horseshoe.

The terrain was rough and they were shielded from the Japs on the hills until they reached the back slopes of Horseshoe.

The laconic sergeant from Utah pushed the squad at a fast clip. He knew Mr. Mac would need help going up the front of that hill.

Crack!

A Jap stuck his rifle out of a burnt-out tank and fired at them. Cherry started to swing his fire team around, to close in on the tank.

"Leave him," Guyman snapped. "We haven't got time — "

Keeping low, they bypassed the tank and the lurking Jap, started along the rear slope of the hill. The reverse side was dotted with caves and bunkers. They shot into them, and threw grenades when they were close enough. Immediately they came under fire.

Cherry, Workman, a rifleman named McLoughlin and Van Camp spread out and began to cut through the side of the hill. Some sort of wide cement ditch or trench pierced the earth at this point and they ran down it, shooting into any hole or bunker mouth they passed.

They were hot and tired, and they threw their shirts away. But they couldn't stop. The Japs had spotted them from distant hills, and the mountain guns on Shuri were being rolled up on their rails to fire. There was one huge monster, apparently an eight-incher, which Cherry called the Okinawa Freight. When one of its shells dropped in, it sounded like the end of the world.

They passed a dark bunker mouth. Someone tossed in a grenade, and they pressed against the walls of the trench, waiting for the explosion, for the black smoke and dust to spurt out.

When the blast came two men leaped forward, spraying the bunker with automatic fire. *Brrrtt! Bam-bam-bam!*

Wheeee — eee-brram!

A 75 mm shell shrieked in at a high angle, almost got Van Camp. He shook his head, his skinny young face tight.

"I wish I'd been a better man," he said to Workman, his foxhole buddy. "You know I caused my mother a lot of trouble — "

"You ain't goin' anywhere, Van," Clyde Workman said.

Rex Guyman was signalling them forward. Rex was a good NCO. He wanted to get on up the hill, take the pressure off the rest of the platoon.

Working by fire teams, the squad spread out along the hillside.

A lot of shell fire was coming in on them, but they had seen only the solitary Jap in the tank. The area around them seemed deserted.

Workman, Van Camp and PFC McLoughlin disappeared from Cherry's view. With PFC Carter and his launcher, he and Bob McCurry were working their way past a dangerous knob overlooking the cement trench.

They heard a spate of rifle and automatic fire a few yards away. Cyde Workman crawled back into their trench, his face working under his close-cropped tow head.

"Van's dead — McLoughlin, too — "

That hit Cherry hard. He and Van had served together in the old Raiders. Van had been a good man, really, only he had never had a chance to clean the slate.

Shaking his head slowly, Cherry heard the long, frightening sigh of the Okinawa Freight coming in. *God*, he thought, *it's coming in right on top of me —*

The big shell had a tremendously high trajectory, and you could hear for ten seconds as it fell. Cherry scrambled along the trench, trying to force himself into a sort of gutter at its side. He passed under the overhanging knob, momentarily forgetting it.

Wheeeee-eee-ka-brrraaam!

The Okinawa Freight crashed into the hillside yards away, doing no damage. At the same time a Jap leaned out from the knob, firing into Cherry's back with a light Nambu. A slug struck him in the pack, went through, and lodged in his spine.

Workman ran up the trench, his M-1 blazing, sheer rage in his clean young face. The Jap screamed and fell, bouncing down the long slope.

Cherry felt no pain, only the stunning blow that had decked him. Now he looked down to his stomach. His belly had suddenly gone loose — all the nerves and muscles in his stomach had let go — but he thought his abdomen was filling with blood.

On Guam he had seen a man shot in the back like this. His stomach had filled with blood, swelling to monstrous size, before the man died.

Cherry was a slim youth — but he looked at the pot appearing under this dirty skivvy shirt and guessed he was dying.

He looked up and saw Rex Guyman's worried face. "Cherry, Clyde got the son-of-a-bitch who shot you. We killed the bastards that got Van, too — "

"Rex, I'm hit," Cherry said. "I think I'm goin' to die. I want you to tell my mother I went out like a man, Rex — " Cherry had tried to move his legs, realized he was paralyzed from the waist down.

Guyman had a syringe of morphine in his hand. All the NCOs carried them.

"Rex, don't put that thing in me. I'm not hurting. I want to go out with a clear head."

Guyman stuck him, anyway. "You ain't going to heaven, Reed — " Then the squad leader stood up, looking at the faces of the men crouching beside him in the trench.

The remnants of the squad were all alone. Guyman realized that the 3rd squad was not going to clear the slopes of Horseshoe. There comes a time when even the old hands have had enough.

"Let's get the hell out of here," the tall man from Utah said. "Somebody pick up Reed's rifle."

They fought their way back down the hill, two of the men carrying the helpless Cherry Reed on a poncho. Cherry said the Twenty-third Psalm out loud. The morphine was getting to him. He began to sing a hymn as Bob McCurry and a man named Walker carried him along.

Walker said, "Reed, you lost your mind?"

"No," Cherry said. "I'm going to make it. I think I'm going to make it now."

They brought him down off the hill three days before his twenty-first birthday. Shortly after that the full battalion went back and tore Horseshoe and Half Moon from Ushijima's desperate, clinging fingers. Shuri was flanked, at last.

In the east, the Army 77th Division, after a battle equal to Sugar Loaf, captured critical Conical Hill. The entire Yonabaru-Naha Line was broken.

By June 30, Okinawa was completely in American hands. A hundred thousand Japanese died. Seven thousand Americans were buried on the island, and thirty-one thousand wounded were evacuated.

Corporal Cherry Reed made it, but he never walked again.

There are no bargains where the price is paid in blood.

After Okinawa all that remained of the great Pacific war was anticlimax.

Japan's Navy lay at the bottom of the ocean. Japan's Army was dead or isolated on countless Pacific islands. Her industry was in ruins, bombed from the bases Marines had secured.

Japan was defeated; the invasion of the home isles was inevitable. A sensible people would have surrendered, but the *Gumbatsu* began to issue bamboo spears to a bewildered but still-trusting peasantry. The course of Ichiki, Saito, Kuribayashi and Ushijima was to be repeated. Understanding this, we can understand a reluctant American government's decision to drop the atom bomb.

This, as nothing else, shocked the *Gumbatsu* from their Oriental delusions. Japan surrendered. Few nations in history had been so thoroughly defeated.

In the closing days of the Pacific War, as in Europe, American policy makers unwittingly were making certain the next conflict would soon take place. The Soviet Union had been coaxed into the war against Japan — after the victory had already been won by American blood.

The Soviet Army poured into Manchuria and Korea, met American troops moving in to try to liberate Japan's conquered provinces.

Korea, an unhappy land long ground under Japan's iron heel, was split in half, the United States occupying the south, the Communists the north. Rival systems of government were set up in each segment of the divided country.

America had defeated a powerful, fanatic enemy. Now, on the ruins of that enemy's former empire, she faced another foe, infinitely worse.

Part Three

A Newer Breed

After the fighting ended in 1945, the Marines finally won another long-sought victory: the Marine Corps mission was defined by law and it included the responsibility for waging amphibious war.

Now there was no question as to the Corps' place in the scheme of things, and it could train and plan with confidence.

But in another sense, the victory was hollow. The Corps was reduced in size, along with the other armed forces. By 1950 there were only some eighty thousand men in Marine green.

Whatever American armed forces may learn on the field of battle — and foreign experts are always amazed at the rapidity with which Americans absorb their bitter lessons — her civilian policy makers never learn that forces in being are a good thing to have around.

They are expensive, true — but not half so expensive as the lives lost because of the too little, too late policy the United States has eternally brought into the opening days of her times of peril.

In 1950, when the Communist-dominated government of North Korea openly attacked the Western-organized regime of the South, the United States could hardly have been less prepared to fight a ground war.

Again the Corps was called — not for amphibious war, but as a fire brigade. And a brigade, at first, was all the Corps could muster.

The Marines, scarce as they were, were forces in being. It was like 1917 again, except that this time the Corps was not detached by executive order. But the Corps had changed since the days of Iwo Jima; less than ten percent of its lower ranks had seen combat. There was some question as to how this newer breed would do.

The decision to commit American forces in Korea had hardly been made before Theater Commander Douglas MacArthur called for Marines. MacArthur already had plans for an amphibious-trained force.

But the plans were to be delayed.

Attacked on June 25, 1950, the Republic of Korea's Army had been shattered within a week by a superior, better-trained and better-equipped Northern Korean Communist Force.

The United States Army divisions, flown in piece-meal from soft occupation duty in Japan, had little better luck. The troops were both physically and psychologically unprepared for combat. The early action in Korea became more and more a precipitous withdrawal.

Finally, four exhausted, battered U.S. and four untrained, lightly armed ROK divisions were trying to hold a hundred and twenty miles of line along the Naktong River west of Pusan against eleven veteran North Korean divisions. There was no place left to which to retreat — at Pusan the sea began.

The Marine Brigade — all the Corps could muster — rushed into the Pusan Perimeter. On the 7th of August, the anniversary of Guadalcanal, it went into action.

The perimeter was like a weakening levee. It was springing leaks. The Marines would be used to plug the holes as they occurred. As the line was slowly pushed back, the brigade rushed up and down along the front, putting out the fires before the house could burn down. It was hot work even for a fire brigade.

Eleven

Bloody Rice: No Name Ridge 1950

"The situation is critical and Miryang may be lost. The enemy has driven a division-sized salient across the Naktong. More will cross the river tonight. If Miryang is lost. . . . we will be faced with a withdrawal from Korea. I am heartened that the Marine Brigade will move against the Naktong salient tomorrow. They are faced with impossible odds, and I have no valid reason to substantiate it, but I have the feeling they will halt the enemy.

. . . . these Marines have the swagger, confidence and hardness that must have been in Stonewall Jackson's Army of the Shenandoah. They remind me of the Coldstreams at Dunkirk. Upon this thin line of reasoning, I cling to the hope of victory." Report wired from Miryang August 16, 1950, by a British military observer to his superiors in Tokyo.

Colonel Chang Ky Dok, commanding the 18th Regiment, 4th Division, North Korean People's Army, was well satisfied with the way things were going. A flat-faced, incisive man, onyx eyes deeply slanted under his cotton military cap, he surveyed his position along Obong-ni Ridge and found it good.

So long as the NKPA held Obong-ni Ridge, the 4th Division's salient across the Naktong appeared safe.

Colonel Chang knew how to evaluate ground from a military viewpoint. Colonel Chang had been around. He'd had formal instruction in a Red Army school in the Soviet Union topped off with combat experience against Chiang Kai-shek while serving in the Chinese Communist forces in North China.

Chang Ky Dok had thus learned what was in the book, and also the way it was done in the field. Along the way, too, like many NKPA officers, he had picked up other things, like using the worst trained and most politically unreliable troops for his first assault wave, reserving the really good men for the second or third when the enemy's ammunition was running out. This was an old Chinese trick, easily assimilated with their tactics of infiltration.

Chang, of course, had added a few purely Korean touches to his military skill. One was the use of refugees. It was an extremely useful tactic to gather a large mob of old men, women, and children and force them toward the American lines while his own men put white robes over their submachine guns and joined the parade.

The other Korean touch was to make the enemy afraid of you. Looking out from Obong-ni, Chang smiled tightly, thinking of the American 25th Division aid stations overrun, the wounded bayoneted as they lay in stretchers. Those mangled dead had been left where they expired, to show the remaining enemy what they could expect.

Crossing the Naktong, Chang's division had badly clawed the U. S. Army's 35th Infantry, forcing it back. Now the NKPA's spies — and there were many — inside the Pusan Perimeter had sent word the infamous Yellow Legs were coming.

In Korea Army GIs wore combat boots, the Marines canvas leggings. At first the NKPA thought the Yellow Legs some kind of foreign troops sent in by the United Nations.

After good dark on August 16, Chang Ky Dok sent for his various battalion and company commanders. He discussed the progress of the war with them, and showed them the three ridge lines dominating the Naktong crossings. All understood the importance of holding this ground against counterattack.

"Our information states we may expect an attack by the Yellow Legs — American Marines," Chang said bluntly. "To us is given the honor of being the first to defeat these Marine soldiers. Where others have failed, we shall conquer."

Chang pointed out over the high ground. "See. They must attack up steep slopes to reach us. Now, go back to your men and inform them there will be no retreat." Chang's dark eyes glittered for an instant in his impassive face. "Tell them I will take instant action against anyone who shows weakness."

The commanders went back and told their men. They did not have to further inform them that in the NKPA instant action usually meant summary execution. The small brown men in the mustard-colored cotton uniforms had discovered this long before.

Roise's 2nd Battalion, 5th Marines, had gotten into Miryang along with the rest of the brigade with just enough time to take a bath in the brown, filthy Miryang River.

They needed it. Mike Shinka's 3rd Platoon of Dog Company was a sad-looking lot after a fortnight in the brown slime of the fecal rice paddies. After they got the dirt and grime washed off, they got a hot meal and new gear. In the few days they had been in the rice paddies of South Korea, exerting themselves under 100 degree heat, their web equipment and dungarees had rotted from their bodies from the constant slime and sweat.

"They are taking too good care of us," PFC Henry Ceniceros, the platoon joker, said. "This is the time you want to watch out — " The young, happy-go-lucky Mexican grinned.

But with new gear and a hot meal, the platoon were a new bunch of men. Sure, their bellies were sweated white from the sullen, constant heat, and their feet and ankles had sores the size of half-dollars from the wet ooze they had lived in — but the States-side and shipboard fat had been sweated off, too, and their faces were bronzed and hard as brown Korean rock. They had been blooded in battle, and they knew this job in Korea wasn't just the herding of a few gooks back on their reservation north of the Parallel. They were up against a tough, vicious foe.

This 17th of August, 1950, moving out from Miryang toward the Naktong, relieving elements of the Army 25th Division, they were a pretty tough lot themselves.

They were going to counterattack the enemy on the ridges overlooking the Naktong crossings. They were either going to save the threatened perimeter or they were going to get their tails shot off.

Maybe, 2nd Lieutenant Michael Shinka, Platoon Commander, thought, *they would do both.*

Dog and Easy Companies of the 2nd Battalion had been signally honored in the early dawn — they had been selected to lead the assault.

By 0700, D and E were in position to see their objective — a long, snake-like ridge spurred by six ugly ribs running down the shale and scrub pine. Neither the rocks nor the trees provided any real cover; the way to the crest of that ridge lay over open ground.

A fresh, ugly landslide scar marked the center of the ridge's spine. Here the reddish brown earth gaped nakedly, and this landmark caused Captain Zimmer of Dog Company to call the ridge "Red Slash Hill." His map wasn't much, and he couldn't pronounce Obong-ni, anyway.

A little farther back, the war correspondents could see the hill, also. They didn't have any kind of a map; when they asked the name of the ridge, someone said, "It ain't got a name."

The correspondents had to write something so they got together and agreed to call it "No Name Ridge." Since their designation and not Andy Zimmer's appeared in the newspapers, No Name Ridge it was.

On the line of departure Captains Zimmer and Sweeney conferred. "I'll take the area right of the red slash," Zimmer said.

"All right, Andy," Sweeney agreed. He would send two platoons up the ridge, alongside the two that would go from Zimmer's Dog Company.

More than that, they didn't have. There were no Marine replacements in Korea, and already the line companies were using technical personnel as rifle fillers.

Shove-off time was set for 0800.

Now, far at sea, the carriers *Badoeng Straits* and *Sicily* turned into the wind. The two Marine air squadrons of MAG-33, their gull-winged Corsairs clumsy with the heavy weight of bombs, roared into the air, sighed over the broken, ugly, brown Korean landscape. Within minutes the planes were over No Name Ridge, blasting it with everything they had.

Bram-braml! Crrump-brram! Bram!

Unfortunately, the Corsairs carried no napalm. But they did the best they could with bombs.

Then the deadly planes rose high and droned away while the ground Marines waited for the artillery to paste the ridge some more. Within seconds the friendly shells were hissing overhead, raising spumes of smoke and dust along the spine of No Name.

Mr. Shinka's 3rd Platoon waited for the preparation to end. They could smell the awful odor of corpses broiled in yesterday's sun — the Army had been forced to abandon their dead as they pulled back. And the 3rd Platoon had passed one Army aid station where the wounded still lay stiffly in their stretchers, stark reminders of the kind of enemy they faced.

But those grotesquely-sprawled, mutilated bodies did not arouse a fear of the North Korean People's Army in Marine breasts. Colonel Chang would have been disappointed — more, he might just have been a little frightened himself, seeing the faces of the passing Marines.

The Marines waiting to jump off were an odd lot. There was big, athletic Sergeant Reese, recalled from mechanic's work at a supply depot to head a rifle squad, then made platoon sergeant of the 3rd. At twenty-one, Dick Reese was one of the oldest men around.

Corporal Baker had become a squad sergeant in Reese's elevation. Walt Baker had been a fireman at Barstow Supply Depot when the call went out for trained Marines. Walt had requested tank duty. He got an M-1.

PFC Lenerd Mateo, half Irish, half Filipino, small and muscular, was a skilled draftsman at a depot in San Francisco when the NKPA came over the 38th Parallel. Since the Corps was going to shoot Communists, not draw pictures of them, Lenerd Mateo got a BAR.

Corporal Robert Hansler was a mechanic, like Reese. He wanted motor transport duty in the Corps. Bob Hansler's BAR-man was Bill McCarver. McCarver had requested pilot training. But he had been an instructor on the rifle range, and the Corps was short of one particular MOS — rifleman.

There were others. Joe Skye, American Indian, who wanted to be an artilleryman, and PFC Phil Lenz, small grinning, well-liked, who wanted to be a farmer when he got out. At seventeen, Phil Lenz figured he had plenty of time. And there was Henry Ceniceros, the platoon joker, who didn't joke when he sighted in an M-1.

This platoon was typical. Nobody in his right mind really wants to be a rifleman — but if a man is a Marine, he is a rifleman first, and whatever interesting little specialty he may pick up along the way comes second.

Against No Name Ridge the artillery shells slammed and burst. McCarver asked sadly, "Why is it we always get the rotten details in the 2nd Battalion?"

"I can tell you," PFC Ceniceros said.

"Yeah? Clue me."

"Sure, I'll give you a clue. Up at regiment the staff officers know we got three battalions. Right?"

"Yeah."

"Now Colonel Murray says to them, 'I'm thinking of a number between one and three —' And they say, 'don't rush us, Colonel — we'll come up with it — hey, we got it! Two?' And there we go again — "

"Aw, for crissakes!"

On No Name the explosions had died away.

"Okay," Mike Shinka said, squinting up toward the ridge. "Let's move out."

They went out in line formation, sloshing across the filthy rice paddies. Dog and Easy Companies — four platoons with 130 men — to attack a thousand. There just weren't any more to throw against the hill.

The 3rd Platoon went across three rice paddies and skirted a field of stunted cotton stalks.

Popopopopopop!

The interior platoon of Easy Company came under fire and slowed. A gap opened between the two assaulting companies.

Brrrrrrrtl Blam-blam-blam!

Fire blazed from the other flank, separating the platoon on the extreme right from Shinka's outfit.

Shinka's platoon was going on ahead of the line now, with flanks exposed. The ground steepened sharply. The riflemen had to scramble up the face of the ridge, panting, bent over. So far no fire had come down from the crest of the ridge, though it whipped in on both flanks from adjoining ridges.

Straining, blowing, Mike Shinka arrived on the crest with twenty men. Here he saw a series of holes which the enemy had dug along the hillside; here also he saw the enemy.

Brrrt-brrrrt-bbrrrrt!

Automatic fire chattered from the right flank, sending the platoon into the holes. And from the reverse slope men in mustard uniforms boiled up, screaming, shouting, firing and throwing grenades.

3rd Platoon could handle them, but it couldn't handle that machine gun fire enfilading it from the right. For a few minutes a crazy, confused fire fight raged along the ridge top as the platoon fired into the men below them. Mateo was hit. Bleeding, he kept firing his BAR, knocked down three shouting Koreans. Henry Ceniceros, brown face set, grabbed the BAR from Mateo as a new knot of NKPA charged the crest. Ceniceros flinched as a bullet struck him, but opened up with the BAR. The NKPA melted away into the ground.

Corporal Bill McCarver realized they had to get out an air panel, point out the location of those enfilading guns to the Corsairs overhead. He jumped out of his hole with a panel. He was struck instantly.

Spurting blood, McCarver, who had wanted to be a pilot, knew the panel had to be put out — but he couldn't do it. In a few seconds, he died.

PFC Lenz, the part-time minister's son, grabbed the panel.

Thwack!

The seventeen-year-old Lenz staggered, dying on his feet. He would never take up farming — he hadn't as much time as he had thought.

Corporal Walt Baker, who liked tanks, saw a straggly bit of brush move to his left. Brush didn't move around on hillsides — even on gook hillsides. He fired his M-1 from his left shoulder.

Crack!

The brush bounced away, tied to a NKPA helmet. The snap shot had gone through the brown face of an enemy soldier trying to flank. Meanwhile, two more men of the platoon were hit by the enfilading fire.

Lieutenant Shinka sweated, looking to the left and right. He was out in front of everybody — nobody was supporting him to either side. There was no way he could get cover from that deadly machine gun fire spurting into his shallow holes. His platoon was being shot to pieces while he watched. It was murder.

"Get the wounded down!" Shinka shouted to Reese, his platoon sergeant. They were going to have to come off the ridge.

The men who could crawl began the painful descent; some were hauled back on ponchos while bullets pecked the earth about them. Halfway down the slope, Shinka found a small gully, and here he gathered in his remaining men. They made the wounded as comfortable as possible.

Then Shinka used his radio, calling the company CP. "We can take the top and hold it," he told Captain Andrew Zimmer, "if you can get that flanking fire off our backs. I've only got fifteen men left. Give me an air strike and some more men. We can make it."

"Negative," Zimmer said. "I can't give you any more men, but I'll get you the air strike right away."

The other platoons making the assault hadn't gotten as far as Shinka. They were all in trouble, and the reserve had gone to help the platoon on Shinka's flank.

While the air strike roared in against the slopes of No Name, Shinka and the other platoon leader coordinated their plans once again. Then the planes buzzed away, and it was up to the riflemen.

They started up the hill again. There were even fewer of them now. The thin, staggering line almost reached the top — then, brown-clad men dashed out of the rear slope, jumped into the holes along the crest where Shinka had tried to make a stand. Rifle fire and grenades met the Marines struggling up the ridge face.

Under the rain of fire and steel the thin line ceased to be a line. Wounded men fell and tumbled all the way back down the steep sides. There were only small knots of green-clad men crawling upward. Fifteen — then eleven — then nine.

Back in the battalion CP a correspondent's face was white. "Good God! How brave can men be?" War Correspondent Jim Bell began to feel ill to his stomach.

Second Lieutenant Mike Shinka got nine men to the top of No Name. He got them into holes filled with the bodies of Korean dead. To his left he saw troops moving in a saddle in the Easy Company zone.

"Easy Company?" he called.

"Yes! Yes!" The answer came in English. Then it was followed by the roar of gunfire. Too late Shinka caught sight of the odd cotton caps framing round, brown heads.

"Son of a bitch — son of a bitch!" Platoon Sergeant Reese yelled, firing into the laughing Koreans with Mateo's old BAR. The NKPA ducked back out of sight.

Today young Mike Shinka was drawing all the hard decisions. Again he was atop No Name, and again he was in deep trouble. He had only Reese and Baker, Cedargren, Smith, and a man named Eric from his own platoon, plus two Marines who had joined from Dog's other platoon.

He was desperately short, but if he could just clear the crest, he could fix it so the adjoining platoons could come up.

The flanking fire he had met before began to chop into his position. He had to go forward or retreat. He couldn't stay where he was. But he was given no time to make the agonizing decision.

Poppopopoppop!

The flanking machine guns went off like popcorn in a kettle. Sergeant Reese rolled in agony. He had been shot through the leg and his thigh was broken. Eric grunted and went down in the open.

Shinka crawled to Eric's side, dragged him back into the faint protection of a shallow hole.

Pow!

The bullet struck Shinka along the jaw. It tore away part of his lower face. He fell back, stunned. When his head cleared, he was choking on his own blood. He leaned over, put his head between his knees, hawking to spit out the strangling blood.

He had a radio, but he could not talk into it to tell Andy Zimmer his situation. But his decision had been made for him. Shinka waved his arm at the anxious faces of his men, motioning them down the hill.

Biting his lips in agony, Platoon Sergeant Reese shook away Walt Baker's helping arm.

"It's okay, Dick. I'll help you down."

"No. I can crawl. You help Eric."

Two of the men pulled Eric onto a poncho, dragged him away to the dubious shelter of the gulley down the face of the ridge.

Behind them, trying to keep from screaming in agony, Sergeant Reese crawled along with his shattered thigh. On the crest Mike Shinka still had something to do. He had to make absolutely certain no wounded Marines were being left behind to the cruel reprisals of the NKPA.

Holding his jaw in place with his left hand, Shinka crawled from body to body, checking eyes, feeling wrists. A hail of bullets still pounded the ridge. As he checked the last sprawled Marine, a slug took Shinka in the right arm.

The impact rolled him halfway down the hill. Shaking his head, gasping for breath through his shattered face, Mike Shinka caught up with Reese. At last, with excruciating agony, they made it into the shelter of the gulley.

A ruuner from Company D CP had arrived there. "Captain Tobin's Baker Company is going to pass through you, Mr. Shinka, and take over."

Shinka, unable to talk, nodded. With his good left hand, he motioned his survivors out of the gulley and back across the fire-swept paddies to the nearest aid station.

Baker Company, as far as Mike Shinka was concerned, could have No Name Ridge. They were welcome to it.

At 1500 in the afternoon, August 17, two relief companies passed through tattered Dog and Easy. They got onto the spurs. But when darkness came, Colonel Chang's 18th Regiment, NKPA, still held Obong-ni. He had suffered six hundred casualties, but he had been reinforced from other units. He knew that the shattered 2nd Battalion had been replaced by the fresh 1st, and this filled him with a good feeling. He knew a great deal. Colonel Chang Ky Dok had a captured American SCR 300 — Signal Corps Radio — tuned in on the Marine battalion's command net.

He knew the weak points where the unit flanks were tied in because the Marines did a great deal of talking over the radio. Happily, he ordered a counterattack to be launched at 0230, August 18.

During August, 1950, there were just not enough good, strong men in the Marine Corps, nor enough on No Name Ridge. Only raw courage and sheer fighting ability allowed the embattled 1st Battalion to hold the ground that had been gained during the precarious hours till the dawn of August 18.

Half of the men who had seen the evening sun go down were gone when that same sun rose in the east. With dawn, the depleted companies still had the job of taking No Name Ridge. The dug-in NKPA machine guns still fired, and to advance was to die. But now the Marines knew where the guns were.

Captain John Stevens called for an air strike. It was a desperate measure. He wanted it very close to his own men. His colonel argued with him.

There was an unofficial rule in the Corps. For a hundred pound bomb, 100 yards of clearance were adequate; for a two hundred pounder, 200 yards. Stevens wanted a five hundred pounder almost on top of his men.

"Colonel, I can't go forward against those guns. It'll cost men to withdraw. I'll get my men in holes. We've got to take the risk." "All right." The Colonel talked to the Forward Air Controller.

The pilots took no chances. They made a dummy run, then one of them marked the tarket. A minute later a 500-pound bomb whistled down upon the narrow crest of the hill.

Brrroooom!

Through the smoke and falling rock, Steven's Able Company pushed forward. They counted four NKPA machine guns knocked out. Nine minutes after the smoke had cleared they had the hill. Even then it had not been without cost. One Marine rifleman had been killed by the bomb blast.

Mopping up the ridge, the Marines found eighteen heavy machine guns, some Russian, some American, and they captured twenty-five light machine guns. There were also some sixty submachine guns left scattered along the ridges, besides piles of grenades and ammunition.

Behind the 1st Battalion, Lieutenant Colonel Taplett's fresh 3rd went into the fight. As the ridges over the Naktong fell, the salient across the Naktong became a death trap for the NKPA 4th Division, and for Colonel Chang Ky Dok. The perimeter had been saved.

It was hot work in the fire brigade. Firemen, particularly when there are not enough of them, get burnt.

A few days after the 1st Marine Brigade sailed for Korea, President Truman authorized the calling up of Organized Reserves.

The Marine Corps has been criticized for its actions in calling its ground reserves, but the Joint Chiefs of Staff had ordered the Corps to place a full division at MacArthur's disposal by September, 1950. The Corps, with only 80,000 men scattered around the world, had no choice. More than 10,000 reservists were ordered into the newly formed 1st Division whose 1st Brigade was already fighting in Korea.

To the younger men, who had joined since the War, it was high adventure. To the veterans who had been on Iwo and Okinawa, mobilization came as more of a blow. They left budding businesses, new wives, young children — and they had given much already.

But any Marine, regular or reserve, is a wise man if he has his bags packed and his last will and testament up to date.

In fifty-three days, by calling regulars and reserves from all across the earth, the 1st Division reached a strength of 23,000. Some men would go into combat without thorough training or retraining. Forces in being are admittedly expensive. But they can never be so expensive as the men who die because they are not in existence or available when the bugles blow.

On September 15, 1950, General MacArthur loosed his master stroke: a push from the strengthened Pusan Perimeter coordinated with a surprise amphibious assault by the 1st Marine Division at Inchon, taking the enemy in the rear from the west.

The Inchon landings were a bold maneuver. The Marines went in on thirty-foot tides to attack a built-up city of 250,000. But the assault was a complete success.

After sharp, bitter fighting, the Division pushed inland and entered Seoul, the ROK capital. The NKPA, caught between the advancing Eighth Army from the south and the amphibious assault from the northwest, collapsed. In a matter of days it was destroyed.

The UN Command made the decision to push north across the 38th Parallel to subdue what had been Communist North Korea. The Marines were pulled back from Seoul and sent to the east coast of Korea to land at Wonsan. Before they could assault the port, the ROK Army took it from the south.

Now the war seemed almost over. In the main only guerrilla forces opposed the UN troops sweeping toward the Yalu. From Wonsan, the Marines, as part of the Army X Corps, were ordered to advance northward into the bleak and hostile mountains fringing the Manchurian border.

They marched north into a bitter land.

Then, in the early days of November, 1950, Chinese Communist forces crossed the Yalu and struck the advancing columns. The Eighth Army, in the west, was halted. The X Corps advance stopped while the UN Command considered, in a fog of doubt and uncertainty, their next step. After halting the American onrush, the CCF had disappeared into the Korean mists. Finally, on November 15, the order came to advance again.

November 23 the Marines ate shrimp cocktail, stuffed olives and roast turkey with cranberry sauce, candied yams, fruit salad, fruit cake and mince pie on the shores of a vast reservoir which they called "Frozen Chosin."

That Thanksgiving Day was a festive occasion both in the States and in Korea. The end of the Korean "police action" seemed in sight.

American Intelligence seemed oblivious to the announced Chinese intention to intervene in Korea. There were CCF "volunteers" in Korea, of course, and these were being mopped up. Perhaps because air reconnaissance saw few Chinese across the icy wastes of far north Korea, UN officers discounted the persistent reports of their presence made by the ROKs.

What American officers did not know was that Chinese armies marched by night, holed up by day. Air could not spot them, nor, in the brutal mountains, could it stop them once they were spotted.

Each day at dusk the hills and valleys of North Korea became alive with mustard-green clad Chinese, marching southward, singing in the wailing minor keys of Mongol music, carrying vast stores of arms and ammunition across the ridges. The nights now were very long and when dawn came the tough, leathery-skinned peasant soldiers crawled into caves and holes, warming their gloveless hands in the sleeves of bulky quilted jackets.

The officers of the CCF were veterans of twenty years of war. They were not fools. They knew exactly what they intended to do in the frozen wastes around the Chosin Reservoir. One job was to destroy the 1st Marine Division.

On November 27, starting a new attack, the Marines discovered there were still plenty of shooting days left till Christmas.

Some of the bitterest fighting in the entire history of land warfare now began.

Twelve

The Savage Land: Crisis at Yudam-ni 1950

To embark on a winter campaign in the land of the Mongols is to invite disaster. Attributed to Genghis Khan.

North from the Korean port of Hungnam facing on the cold, gray waters of the Japan Sea rises a narrow, winding road of gravel and dirt. This road, for the first part of its existence — the forty-three miles from Hungnam to Chinhung-ni — has two lanes and moves through reasonably rolling hills and flat plain. Traveling the road this far is not unpleasant.

North from Chinhung-ni all pleasure ends. The remaining thirty-five miles to the sordid little hamlet of Yudam-ni are a multiple nightmare.

At Funchilin Pass, between Chinhung-ni and Koto, the ground rises 2500 feet into thin mountain air. The road now is only a single-lane twisting ribbon with a precipice on one side and a yawning abyss on the other.

The forlorn town of Koto-ri is set in the midst of a rugged plateau. From this plateau the road creeps through mile-high hills to the city of Hagaru at the southern tip of the vast Chosin Reservoir.

Hagaru, an important center before the War, huddles in a bleak natural amphitheater of six square miles. From it the road turns northwest, skirting the reservoir. After fourteen miles, after it has climbed the 4,000-foot peaks of Toktong Pass, it comes down through sullen gorges to a broad valley ringed by five great ridges.

In this valley, 3,500 feet above sea level, while the peaks surrounding it rise almost a mile into the bitter wind, lies the miserable village of Yudam-ni which is a road junction. It is not much else, even to the people who live there.

The country through which this tortuous road winds is bleak and barren in winter, and winter comes early. The hills are brown and bare; what dead grass remains rustles dead and sere. There are repeated snowfalls and ice covers the forlorn passes and craggy ridges. The wind blows constantly and the cold is intense and bone-chilling.

The maps do not indicate such arctic weather; Yudam-ni is not so far north. But there is nothing to stop the Siberian winds that howl off the roof of the world and scream across the frozen Yalu from the land of the Mongols.

This small stretch of road, 78 miles in all, has no real name. In November, 1950, Americans called it the MSR. The Main Supply Route. But all Marines know what the words *the MSR* mean — as though there were never any other.

Up this road in November, 1950, came the 1st Marine Division. It was not together — it could not move together. The 5th and 7th Marines pushed far ahead, taking the hills around Yudam-ni; behind them they left a battalion and supporting troops in Hagaru to build an air strip. Fox Company of the 7th remained in Toktong Pass to protect the road. Far behind, the 1st Marines' RCT pushed into Koto-ri.

Three regimental combat teams of Marines, with sundry Army troops, were spread over many miles of Korean landscape, joined only by a fragile and tortuous thread — the MSR. To their east the closest friendly troops were the soldiers of the ROK and the 7th Army Division, marching along the east coast and now reaching the Yalu.

To their west, the Eighth Army was eighty miles away, separated by horrendous mountains. What lay within that eighty-odd miles, no one knew. The terrain was such that it was impossible to find out.

Veteran Marine officers were not easy or confident about the aspects of this march north. Old China hands recalled the bitter snows of Manchuria. The exposed tactical position was obvious to a second-year ROTC student.

But the Marine Division, like the rest of the troops in Korea, had their orders: press on to the Yalu and end the war.

They pressed on.

General Sung Shih-lun was a hard-headed capable officer whose icy efficiency was marred only by a quick temper. At seventeen he had departed the Whampoa Military Academy to fight for the Communists, and he had been commanding men in battle ever since. In November, 1950, the Chinese Year of the Tiger, Sung Shih-lun was forty years of age.

A small, parchment-colored man With slanted obsidian eyes, Sung was famed as one of the three bravest men in the CCF. He was given command of the 9th Army Group, totalling one hundred thousand men.

The units under Sung's command were accustomed to victory. They had both pride and tradition. They had little equipment, but leaders such as Sung Shih-lun knew how to make up for that.

The CCF employed massive infiltration, double envelopment, isolation and piecemeal destruction of isolated units. Its custom was to probe the enemy until it found a soft spot, then flail this spot until the opposing lines broke. The Chinese units were mobile — minds influenced by the vast expanse of China cannot think in terms of static positions.

General Sung Shih-lun knew as much of Clausewitz as any Western commander. If his tactics differed from European thinking, it was only because he took into account the type of soldier he commanded.

The Chinese peasant soldier is tough. He eats very little and hardship is his accustomed lot. He is as brave as any soldier in the world, and he is well-indoctrinated. In China battle fatigue is not recognized.

Now, in November, 1950, Sung Shih-lun marched his hordes down from the Yalu in fourteen days. It was a prodigious feat to cross the icy mountains. Artillery had to be abandoned, but the soldiers themselves arrived near the Chosin Reservoir in good condition.

At Paemyangji-san, ten miles north of Yudam-ni, General Sung Shih-lun established his headquarters. Here he told his officers: "Soon we shall meet the American Marines in battle. We shall destroy them. Kill these Marines as you would snakes in your homes."

Sung had adequate intelligence of the movements of the Americans at a time when the UN had no idea of where the CCF were, or what they would do.

Sung knew a massive blow would be launched against the Eighth Army in the west, then his own troops would envelop the Marine Division and destroy it.

The Marines were strung out over miles of ground, linked only by a fragile mountain road. They were isolated in deep mountains. They were far from home and far from help. He gave orders for his divisions to infiltrate over the mountains and cut the American MSR. Hagaru and Koto-ri would be taken, hit from the flanks and rear. The road would be blocked in a dozen places. Chinese troops would dig in along the hills beside the American escape route.

The two regimental combat teams near Yudam-ni, once isolated, could be pounded to fragments and dissolved.

It was a very good plan — one which the UN Command had given an excellent chance of success by its maneuver.

As the swollen, gibbous moon rose over the harsh frozen landscape of the land of the Mongols, Sung Shih-lun gave his final orders. They were understood, and they were obeyed. Any man who did not obey instantly was cured permanently of such hesitation by the application of a pistol muzzle to the back of his skull.

The hills swarmed with black figures. Whistles and horns called the fighting hordes to the kill. Soon there would be warm blood on the icy earth, freezing slowly in the cold rays of the moon.

As night fell November 27th, the men of Mr. Yancey's Platoon, Easy Company, 7th Marines had prepared their positions on Hill 1282, just north of Yudam-ni. Digging in had been pure torture, PFC Clue Jackson thought. Under the steep, snow-covered ridges the earth was deep-frozen, and every man in the company was exhausted to the bone. Without the labor of climbing ridges and digging frozen foxholes, the chill alone was enough to sap a man's will.

God, the cold — the everlasting cold! The first blast of it a few days before had hit the Marines as a shock. Men were dazed, incoherent; some cried with the pain and numbness of it. The parkas and shoepacs didn't keep it out. Feet slowly froze and soon each step was agony.

Clue Jackson rubbed his black-bearded, stiffened cheeks with an aching hand. *God, his feet hurt!* Every time he moved the sudden bite of pain brought tears to his smarting eyes. A little drop of mucus ran from his hooked nose, dribbled onto his thin lips, freezing solid.

He was hungry. All the cans of C-rations he carried had frozen, and the icy food brought severe stomach cramps if he tried to eat it. The water in his canteen froze, unless he kept the container inside his jacket. For a couple of days Clue had had only dry dog biscuit from the canned rations and a candy bar to eat.

The attacks this 27 November hadn't gone too well, Clue knew. Everywhere, the Marine units trying to move west had been repulsed. Easy Company hadn't had much contact so far although they had bagged one Chink officer.

The Chinaman had carried a plotting board, an alidade, and a tape measure. *Jesus*, Clue Jackson thought again, *was the bastard going to measure us?*

Like half the men around him, Clue was a reservist. Yeah, he'd gone that route after the big war. He hadn't kept active, either, so he'd make more rank. This company wasn't veteran, but it was learning.

As the darkness pushed over the barren, jagged hills, Captain Phillips and Lieutenant Yancey made sure the company was prepared. Yancey's boys were atop the hill, facing northeast. Other platoons formed crescents, facing in all directions. In the center of the half circles, Phillips set up his CP and his mortars.

It was about a thousand yards over to the next hill where Dog Company dug in. Hill 1282 was kind of lonely.

Lieutenant John Yancey was a veteran, though, from the old Raider battalions. He set up his machine guns to cover the approaches, went about seeing that the men were ready and stayed that way.

Something was in the wind as the sun went down, and it was more than Chinese bugles.

The distant haunting sound drifted across Hill 1282 from the north. There was something spine-chilling about it.

Tatatatatatataaaaa! Craaa! Craaa!

This was no call any of the Marines recognized.

Pvt. Jim Gallagher worked the bolt of his light machine gun. He was a capable man who had proved himself at Sudong. "Make that moon come over the mountain, Mac," he said.

Clue Jackson said, "I'll give you a clue. Moonrise is at 1810."

"Lot of good it'll do — the mist is rising."

Further along the hill, Mr. Yancey was talking to Pvt. Stan Robinson whose frost-bitten feet were a mass of bloody flesh. "Robinson, get your ass back to the medical tent."

"Aw, no, goddamnit," Robinson argued. "I can walk!" But Yancey took his BAR away. Cursing unhappily, Robinson began to limp back toward the warmth of the tents at Yudam-ni.

At 1810 the moon showed — lopsided, ugly, four days past full. It threw ghastly moon-shadows over the gaunt peaks, gleaming sullenly through the overcast. It was a bloody moon, Clue thought.

Soon there was light gunfire, and scattered probing along the base of the hill. It was nothing the men on the hill couldn't handle. Gradually, then, the silence around the hill deepened.

"What the hell is that?" Gallagher, Clue and the men around them suddenly stiffened, listening. Mr. Yancey turned his ear to the north.

It sounded like thousands of boots stamping in the snow. It was approaching through the dark.

"Damn, I hope this gun hasn't frozen," Gallagher muttered.

Clue had put Vaseline hair tonic on the bolt of his own M-1. All the Vaseline and Wildroot in the company had gone for gun grease. The regular oil froze solid, and even the lighter hair tonic had to be put on very lightly.

On Hill 1282 the temperature had dropped to twenty below.

Mr. Yancey spoke into his field phone, calling Lieutenant Ball, Easy's Exec. "Give us some flares with the 81s, then lay in and work back."

Ball, in charge of the mortars, answered, "We're short of 81s. We can't give you many."

"Oh, goddamn," Mr. Yancey said.

Coming up the ridge, in long thin lines, were wavering shadows. Wave after wave of shadows fifteen yards apart and slowly advancing.

"Trip the flares!"

The ghastly lights popped into the air. As far as the light threw its searching glare, Clue saw Chinese. Long, widespread lines of them, hunched over, moving toward 1282.

As the flares popped, the Chink bugles blared; the horns and whistles shrieked for the kill.

Craaaz — crass! Tatatatataaaa!

The noise made the night hideous under the ghostly moon.

And the Chinese were chanting.

"Son of a bitch-Marines!
We kill.
Son of a bitch — Marines!
You die!"

"Lay it on, Ray — lay it on!" Mr. Yancey screamed to Ball over the wire.

"Let the bastards have it!" Gallagher tripped the firing studs on his light thirty and the night exploded into flame.

Blam! Blam! Blam! Blam!

The mortars burst in front of the Marine positions, slamming their sharp explosions through the sound of small arms fire.

Mr. Yancey moved about, directing the fire.

Blam!

A Chinese grenade blew up in his face; a fragment cut through his nose. Blood began to run down inside his mouth and throat; Yancey spit it out, kept on with his job.

Captain Phillips ran to Yancey's platoon. They were catching the brunt of the attack; he brought extra ammunition. Immediately he was hit by rifle bullets in shoulder and leg. He ignored the hurts.

"You're doing okay, men! Stay loose — you're doing okay!"

Taraaa! Tafatatataraaa!

It was too hot in front of the hill; the Chinese bugles sang the recall. Leaving heaped piles of dead in the snow, the assaulting waves withdrew.

A dead Chink sprawled twelve feet in front of Clue. He blew on his red, stiff hands, stamped his feet before he remembered — *ohh, God!*

But at least his rifle was warm. He hunched over it.

A hospital corpsman tried to bandage Phillips' wounds while he got on the horn to Battalion. "Colonel, we broke up the first attack but we've taken a lot of casualties. We may need help."

"Okay, boy. I'll get it up to you."

The colonel sent two more platoons from another company up the hill. The wounded and dead on Hill 1282 were brought down. Then, slowly freezing, eyes smarting as they strained into the weird night, Clue and the other men of Yancey's platoon waited.

Some of the wounded were carried into the warm blast of the hospital tents on the floor of the valley. Lying in his sleeping bag, Private Stanley Robinson had heard the wild popping of the fight on 1282. Now he asked a bleeding man the stretcher bearers brought in, "What outfit you from?"

"Easy, 7th Marines."

"Did we get hit?"

"God, we got clobbered. Mr. Yancey's wounded. Skipper, too. I guess everybody's wounded."

Robinson got up, felt for his parka and shoepacs. He almost screamed as the cold boots went over his blood and pus-streaked feet. Then he stood erect.

"So long, Mac," he groaned to the other man from Easy Company. Gasping, groaning, he reached for a rifle in the discarded stack outside the tent. A corpsman yelled at him.

"Where the hell you goin', Robinson?"

"What's it look like, Doc?"

"Get back in your sack!"

"Get out of my way."

Robinson slung the rifle on his shoulder and headed back for beleaguered Hill 1282.

He found Mr. Yancey spitting blood in the snow. "What in hell are you doing back here?" Yancey croaked.

Robinson said angrily, "Looking for a job."

Yancey looked at him. Then he cleared his throat again of blood. "You got one." He motioned Robinson into a hole near Clue.

In the valley the monstrous, shuffling sound advanced again.

Tatatatatataa! Taraaaa! Taraaa!

Son of a bitch, Marines.

You die!

"Oh, crud!" Clue Jackson mumbled, firing steadily as the Chinese waves whipped at the scant line of holes dug along the ridge.

This time there was no stopping them. Small, bulky men in padded jackets catapulted into the perimeter. Rifle and machine gun fire streaked in all directions as Easy desperately tried to repair the breaks and stem the tide.

Mr. Yancey took another grenade fragment in the mouth, kept on shouting orders. The company skipper ran forward, shouting.

"Hold on, men! Hold on! This is Easy Company!"

The skipper took a rifle from a dead Marine and hurled it bayonet-first into the icy ground. The bayonet went into the earth, and the rifle butt swayed back and forth in the wind, a marker of defiance, a flag to rally on.

"Easy Company holds here!"

Still shouting, Captain Phillips died beside his improvised flag.

Lieutenant Ball, the exec, was already wounded. He could not move, but he tried to rally the dissolving perimeter, firing a rifle repeatedly into the the on-pressing Chinese. He was hit, then hit again. He collapsed and bled to death.

All over the hill, in other units, the fighting reached insane fury.

Clue fed his last clip into the hot magazine of his M-1, triggered it steadily at the short, quilted figures stumbling into the company CP.

Brrangg!

The empty clip flew out of his rifle.

The platoon was down to nine men. Mr. Yancey, still on his feet, was yelling for a counterattack. With a bayonet and bad feet Clue, Robinson and Gallagher started forward behind the platoon leader.

Yancey could barely talk through the bleeding in his throat.

He gasped the old Raider Battalion's rallying cry: *Gung Ho!*

Oh, hell, Clue Jackson thought. "Gung Ho!" he croaked.

They started forward with bayonets against the milling, disorganized Chink horde that swarmed the hill. There was a vicious volley of Chink fire. Metal sliced into Mr. Yancey's right cheek. He fell down, blind. On his knees he tried to crawl forward into the Chinks ranks.

It was hopeless. Under vicious fire, the remnants of the platoon hit the ground, drawing away in the dark.

But the fight was not over. More Marines charged up the hill from the 5th Marines and threw the Chinese back. Just as day streamed over the white, frozen mountains they swept the enemy off the crucial ridge, took it and held it.

Clue and the other survivors of Easy Company came out of their holes to join the new unit. All day, under heavy pressure, they stayed on the hill. More than two hundred wounded were carried down its slopes.

Late that afternoon Jackson, Gallagher, Robinson and about twenty others still alive from Easy's one hundred-and-eighty men were told to come down off the hill as a new company relieved them.

All around Yudam-ni it had been the same. The MSR was cut and Fox Company was holding off overwhelming numbers of attackers back in Toktong Pass. The battalion guarding the base at Hagaru was keeping the Chinese at bay with artillery fire alone in some sectors.

Everywhere the icy hills vomited Chinese, gunfire, and death. But everywhere, like Easy Company, 7th Marines, the leathernecks held. Freezing, bleeding and dying, they held.

Tactically the Chinese Communists forces were inflicting a defeat on the Marines. They had blocked their advance, surrounding them, cut them off from help — except by air. Now it seemed to tacticians across the world, listening to the news that the CCF could gobble up the Marines at leisure.

Stateside, the newspapers and radio dispensed finely distilled gloom. Some said it would be the worst defeat in U.S. history.

In Yudam-ni, in Hagaru, in Koto and safe and warm in the supply base at Hungnam, the officers knew the Marines would have to come back out of the hills of North Korea. In the west Eighth Army was hard hit by other Chinese armies and in retreat. All UN forces would have to pull south; they had not been prepared for the massive Chinese intervention.

But a move to the rear is not always a defeat.

While the 1st Division — every man a rifleman — battled for survival, General Oliver Smith, its commander snorted, "Retreat, hell! We're going to attack in a new direction."

With officers like Captain Phillips and Lieutenant Yancey at their head, and with men in the ranks like Robinson, Gallagher and limping re-tread Clue Jackson, the Chinese themselves were in trouble.

As PFC Jackson said later, "Somebody should've clued those bastards in. They were the jokers who had the tiger by the tail!"

As the Year of the Tiger waned, both Marines and the CCF were astride the tiger's back. The world waited while the agony in the hills of North Korea continued.

Battling almost five-to-one odds, the Marine Division fought off attack after attack. They held their bases at Yudam-ni, Hagaru and Koto-ri. But their thin life line — the MSR — was cut. They were encircled on all sides. The question was whether or not they were trapped.

The supply situation, and that of the hundreds of wounded, was extremely serious. It was obvious that the Marines would have to move south. Litzenberg's 7th RCT and Murray's 5th were surrounded at Yudam-ni; another battalion, plus service troops, was under siege at Hagaru. Puller at Koto could not bull his way through to them.

Marine, Navy and Far Eastern Air Force planes blackened the wintry skies over Hagaru, blasting ridges, dropping ammo, spotting lurking enemy groups. Without those planes, the Marines, indeed, would have been without hope. At Hagaru a landing strip was rushed to completion.

Between Yudam-ni and Hagaru rose treacherous Toktong Pass, its gloomy chasms dark with Chinese, its fourteen miles a hellish gantlet of fire. Atop Toktong, Barber's Fox Company, 7th, still held out against incredible pressure, but it was cut off from both camps.

The first step was for the encircled Marines to blast their way out of Yudam-ni, relieve Barber at Toktong, then bring the two RCTs into Hagaru and its air strip. If they could.

Thirteen

Death on the Ridges: Toktong Pass 1950

"We've been looking for the enemy for several days. Well, we've finally found them. We're surrounded. That simplifies our problem of killing them." Colonel Lewis "Chesty" Puller, commanding 1st Marines, Koto-ri, to newsmen November, 1950.

On the floor of the Yudam-ni plateau shattered units of the besieged Marines were being reorganized. Captain Phillips' Easy Company, 7th Regiment, consisted of thirty men; Hull's Dog Company was joined with it, making a total of seventy-five effectives. To this nucleus came a hundred cannon cockers from the artillery battalions and the 7th's Weapons Company. When they put it all together, it wasn't much, but they called it a battalion. Major Roach, regimental supply officer, was placed in charge.

When Major Roach reported in by field phone, he used a new call sign: "This is Damnation Six — "

Units that badly shot up should have been in despair, unable to go back into action. But Clue Jackson, Privates Robinson and Gallagher found a torn parachute from an air drop, and made green scarves which they draped around their necks. Immediately, every man in the new provisional battalion did the same.

Damnation Battalion had been born.

"I'll give you a clue," PFC Jackson said to anyone who cared to listen. "We're gonna blast our way outa this place."

"Why not?" Someone answered him. "We got twenty-six shooting days till Christmas."

Limping but confident, Damnation Battalion marched to the perimeter to hold the high ground the rest of the 7th had to move through on its way to Toktong Pass.

But Damnation Battalion was in no shape to handle the hard job — that of blasting across the mountains to Hagaru. That fell to Lieutenant Colonel Raymond Davis' 1st Battalion.

At the CP tent in Yudam-ni Colonel Litzenberg talked to Davis on November 29. "We've got to relieve Barber at Toktong Pass."

Litzenberg had bold scheme. He wanted Davis to take his battalion across the mountains at night. "It's obvious we can't bull our way down that road. I don't think the Chinese will expect us to move overland. Prepare to move out tomorrow morning."

When the word was passed to Davis' men, Cpl. Henry Jasko said, "Why not? If the Chinks can run the goddamn ridges, why can't we?"

In Korea men were not asking *why?* Everywhere it was *why not?*

Jasko, his olive-skinned face chapped by the cold but his dark brown eyes calm in his round face, helped get the march organized. Any man on his feet was due to go. The wounded and sick would stay behind but they weren't relieved of duty. They had to bring out the battalion vehicles and equipment once the road was cleared.

Every man was given rations for four meals, a canteen of water and extra ammo. In addition to his regular weapons and gear, each Marine had to carry one 81mm mortar shell and his sleeping bag.

In the hills those mortar rounds would be needed — and in the hills an immobilized Marine without his arctic bag would quickly freeze.

It was twenty-four degrees below zero as they moved out.

Henry Jasko marched with the lead company. For twenty days he had been existing in subzero temperatures, and he had forgotten his last hot meal. He knew he had lost weight, maybe fifteen pounds, because his trousers were loose and there was lots of room under his jacket for three cans of fruit. With his tin of bread — dog biscuit — that was his day-and-a-third's ration.

His stubby, brown hands were cut and bloody from scrabbling in the frozen earth and the right side of his face felt stiff from frostbite. But what the hell, he didn't have to shave for awhile yet.

1st Battalion, 7th, went into the hills. A thousand yards east of the MSR they drew fire from a hill shown on the maps as 1419.

Hill 1419 had to be taken so they methodically went about attacking it.

The Chinese were entrenched across the hill; Colonel Davis called for artillery from Yudam-ni and air strikes. While the crest was wreathed in smoke, three companies assaulted.

This is a hell of a charge, Jasko thought, *Climbing up on our hands and knees.*

Whap! Whap!

Mortar fire lashed the slopes as they ascended. Grimly they continued the difficult, hazardous climb. Several times heavy fire pinned them down, but on one side or the other Marines smashed through to take off the pressure. Then they broke over the crest. Chinese whirled in their holes. In a wild melee Henry Jasko shot down two with his M-1.

Brrrrrt!

A Chink fired at him with a high cyclic rate burp gun — one of the Russian-made Tommy guns the Chinks carried. The Chink ducked back behind a ridge.

Henry hit the deck. He wasn't going after the Chink. He didn't need to. He pulled the pin on a grenade, lobbed it high over the ridge.

Bum!

The explosion echoed off the hills amid the spatter of automatic fire. The Chink bounced up from behind the fold of ground, rolled a long way before he stopped.

Then, suddenly, there were no more Chinks. Henry helped carry the dead and wounded Marines down from the hill; they would be hauled back to Yudam-ni. After this, now that they were leaving the proximity of the road, the dead and wounded would have to be carried, along. Things had to be pretty bad before Marines left their own behind.

By the time they had secured the hill mass, it was past dark. Henry felt the chill wind cutting into him as the sun went down — he had sweat underneath his winter garments and now his ass felt as if it had ice on it.

Jeez, we'll freeze to death up here, he thought, even in our sacks.

Lieutenant Colonel Davis, who didn't often think like Henry, had the same idea. The temperature continued to drop and Davis realized his tired, sweaty Marines, listless after a day of hard combat up the hill, might never get up again if he allowed them to bed down.

He ordered Henry's company to scout ahead and report back. They did so, but saw no signs of enemy troops.

His stubbled face determined, Ray Davis decided there was only one thing to do — go on. He took out a poncho. In its cover he flipped on his flashlight, reading his compass. When he had his directions straight, he called First Lieutenant Joe Kurcaba, Henry Jasko's company commander.

"See that bright star there in the south — the low one? March on it. I'll follow just behind you with the command group."

In the dark 1st Battalion shoved off again. It was slow, laborious going through the rocks and frozen, dead brush, especially for men in a chronic state of exhaustion. They put the hoods up on their parkas, shielding their faces from the keen wind. Some of them marched with their eyes closed, shutting out the savage land about them.

On a night march men normally think of many things — home, loved ones, pleasures past and hoped-for. Half-sobbing as he plodded forward, Henry Jasko didn't think of anything at all. He was too tired, too, cold, too numb.

On the ridges Joe Kurcaba could see the guiding star. When the column passed down into the valley, he took a wrong turn, veering to his right. Behind him Ray Davis sensed the march was going wrong. He snapped to his radio man, Corporal Pearl, "Contact Kurcaba!"

The radio was frozen — at least it wouldn't even squawk.

"Pass the word," Davis ordered. "Pass the word up the column for Mr. Kurcaba to halt."

The word didn't get past ten men. With their hoods over their ears, sloshing along, they couldn't hear.

Angrily, Davis began to run ahead alongside the stumbling column. "Damn it, men, stay awake. Heads up! Stay alert!"

As he ran by cursing and thrashing in heavy snow, PFC Jasko snapped at him, "Pipe down, damnit! You're making a lot of noise."

Davis caught up with the point. The column stopped. One by one the plodding Marines pushed into the man ahead of them. The men up front were leaden-legged from breaking trail in snow; the men behind them exhausted from trying to keep footing on the ice which quickly formed.

When they realized the column had stopped, they sank down into the snow with loud gasps of relief. They had stopped just in time. Dead ahead of them lay a ridge swarming with CCF.

Rifles and submachine guns blazed and chattered in the freezing night. Officers and sergeants reeling with exhaustion passed along the fallen rows of men, prodding them to their feet. Groaning, the Marines got up and advanced in column. Now the heavy mortar shells they had carried paid off. The battalion mortars vomited a hail of fire and metal on the enemy hill while the reeling Marines charged in two columns.

Once on their feet, nothing could stop Davis' men. They surged forward, swept the Chinese off the ridge in a shooting, shouting wave. Some of the Chinks were asleep or numb with cold. They died, shot to death as they lay, as Marines poured across the frigid hills.

Amid the freezing corpses, the battalion had to halt for reorganization. Davis saw they were collapsing like dominoes in the snow. A file went down, each man pushing the man ahead of him to earth. When a few Marines went down, the urge to lie down was irresistible to the others. Sighing, 1st Battalion collapsed in its collective tracks.

Rifle slugs began whistling off the boulders about them, but not a man moved. They'd had it.

"Damn it, shake the men awake! Form a perimeter. I want at least twenty-five percent of the men alert."

"Jasko, bear a hand! Get your men up!"

Painfully Henry got to his feet. *Who wanted to be a goddamn corporal anyway?* But he was — and with a drugged brain he shook the slumped shoulders about him.

"All right, off your ass!" *Jeez, I don't mind dying — if I could just lie down where it's warm* — "Rise and shine!"

At last, Colonel Davis understood the men had to rest. He looked at his watch — 0300. He decided to linger on this ridge until daylight, enemy fire or not. He got enough men alert to button up the perimeter. His own head was swimming with fatigue; in the numbing cold it seemed to take him a long time to think.

He told Kurcaba and the other company commanders privately, "I want you to check every order I give. If it doesn't make sense, sound off."

A few Marines banged back at the long range small arms fire pinging into the area. The rest were in their sleeping bags, inert.

Jasko and a few others moved about in two-man patrols, making certain enough men stayed awake to protect the huddled battalion.

Davis got out his own sleeping bag and dragged it into the shelter of a rock. He unzipped the bag, threw back the hood. As he did so, a bullet whined from a rock, tore through the bag's hood. It missed Davis by inches.

There comes a time when a man doesn't care. Davis crawled in the bag and zipped it tight, waiting till dawn.

Daybreak December 2 came clear and cold. No one who has not endured sub-zero temperatures in the open under battle conditions can comprehend the effort it took the men of 1st Battalion, 7th Marines, to move out.

Extreme cold itself saps a man, draining his strength. Add the tension of constant danger and the exertion of combat at high altitudes. Add the many days of meager diet of low caloric intake, the frozen foods and resulting dysentery.

It is easy to understand why the CCF failed to believe the Ridge Runners of Toktong Pass could cross the mountains.

And while Davis' men traversed the jagged peaks, 3rd Battalion, 5th Marines, attacked down the MSR, clearing heavy opposition. Item Company shattered itself shortly after midnight against the far side of the same hill mass Davis' men were attacking though neither battalion knew the other's whereabouts.

It took 3rd Battalion — Colonel Taplett commanding — till noon December 2 to clear his side of the hill. The remnants of Dog-Easy Companies, Damnation Battalion, took the place of the decimated Item. Then the 3rd continued to fight its way along the MSR to Hagaru.

With the coming of daylight Davis' men were up and moving stiffly to the attack. Carrying their own wounded in stretchers, firing their weapons as they struggled upward, they cleared Hill 1653. They knew they were close to where Fox Company should still be holding out, but no radio contact could be made.

The brief rest had given new strength to Corporal Henry Jasko — strength he never dreamed he had. Plunging up the hills, firing and fired at, he seemed to have found second wind, a new life. With all the men around him it was the same. Only the wounded were in bad way.

Light-headed, legs shaking, the Marines hit the Chinese on the hilltops with a savagery the CCF could not match. The horrible climate was numbing the enemy, too. But the biggest weapon, Jasko realized, was surprise. The Chinks just didn't think they'd had it in them.

They attacked a new hill, driving the Chinese off in a rattle of rifle and machine gun fire. As Henry and his fire team sank down on the hard rock, feeling the sweat freeze between their thighs, Colonel Davis came up the slope.

Behind him his radio man, Pearl, began to shout. "Colonel, I've got Fox Six on the radio!"

Barber's beleaguered F Company was on the next hill. As the cutoff company commander talked with Davis, his voice began to shake with emotion. Captain Barber had been through five days and nights of incessant battle. Only one of Fox Company's seven officers was unhurt; the company had suffered 26 killed and 89 wounded. Three men were missing. The handful who were left all had frostbite and rampant dysentery.

Talking to Barber, Davis' own voice began to shake. For a minute neither officer could talk coherently.

Then, carrying their 22 wounded, Davis' men joined Fox on the hill. Toktong Pass was clear!

At 1300 the first tanks came down the road from Yudam-ni. Davis received new orders from Litzenberg: *Assume the point and lead the way to Hagaru.*

Overhead Davis and Jasko noticed that the skies were filled with gull-winged Marine Corsairs, manned by pilots who were also ground officers and clearly understood what the men below were going through.

The Corsairs napalmed and rocketed the mountains along the road until the earth itself shook. They drove the weary CCF from the peaks. Some were seen fleeing. Some threw away their arms and lay huddled together in the snow for warmth where the Marines came upon them.

The hardy Chinese peasant, used to hardships all his life, had broken while the Marine pride and *esprit de corps* had seen them through.

Behind Davis' fighting patrols came the vehicles and the walking wounded. Only men who were too badly hurt to move at all were allowed to ride. No one complained.

At 1900, December 3, the point broke into the wide, windy plateau of Hagaru. Several hundred yards from the Hagaru's defenders' position, the column stopped. No one said anything; like Jasko, they were too tired to speak.

But now every man who could stand formed on the frozen plain in the full view of the Hagaru defenders. They started forward, and somehow, without an order being spoken, they began to march in cadence.

The eyes of the Marines of Hagaru who had been through their own nights of fire filled with tears. Someone said, over and over again: "Look at those bastards — look at those magnificent bastards!"

The Marines of Yudam-ni and Hagaru had joined.

The almost three thousand wounded and injured could be flown out from the air strip. Now the encircled Marines, relieved of their wounded and resupplied, could prepare to fight their way out to the sea, bringing their equipment with them.

They were still cut off. They were still surrounded by hills swarming with Chinese. They were a long way from home. But they were no longer on the defensive. They had seized the initiative and would never let it go. North Korea had to be abandoned, but they would abandon it like men, like United States Marines!

From General Smith to Colonel Litzenberg, from Lieutenant Colonel Davis to Henry Jasko and Clue Jackson, ran a common thought:

We're coming out. There aren't enough Chinese upon this earth to beat us now.

The Marines came out. They came out with their wounded, most of their equipment and with their heads up.

Tactically they had been defeated. They had given up ground. But the CCF, surveying a wasteland littered with the corpses of their men, had good reason to question the quality of their victory. Never again, however, would they question the quality and fighting ability of United States Marines.

In the spring of 1951 the tide turned again. UN Forces made a stand, won revenge for the losses in the north. Again the American tide surged up the Korean peninsula, reaching the 38th Parallel, passing it. Shattered, the Chinese armies retreated.

When Communists sense victory at arms, they fight. When they cannot win, their tactic is to talk until the time is ripe to fight once more. The CCF asked for a truce.

The UN agreed to talk. While a cease-fire was debated, the CCF and the Eighth United States Army Korea faced each other across heavily defended lines. The debate, once begun, continued endlessly.

And so did the war. But now it was a war of position, not movement, as each side tried to improve its defensive lines. Battles erupted over hills and outposts as the CCF tested the Americans' nerve again and again.

Before the final cease fire came in July, 1953, the Marines, part of EUSAK, saw plenty of action. As, for example, the action at Carson, Reno and Vegas. . . .

Fourteen

Outpost: Reno, 1952

Forward of the MLR occupied and defended by the 2nd Bn 7th Marines, three combat outposts are maintained on certain prominent terrain features. These outposts . . . CARSON, RENO and VEGAS, serve to maintain a line of contact with the enemy well forward of the MLR. . . . Staff Memo, 2/7, 1st Marine Div (Reinforced) FMF In the Field 1 November 1952.

Carson, Reno and Vegas were well forward, all right. They were so damned far forward of the Marine main line of resistance that Mack Tareau, Operations Officer of the 2nd Battalion, figured holding them at all was going to be a precarious gamble.

With this in mind, Major Tareau suggested to Lieutenant Colonel Anthony Caputo, the tall, dark, balding battalion C.O., that the names Reno, Carson and Vegas be made official. Caputo's white teeth flashed as he considered it.

"How about Elko or Monte Carlo, Mack?"

"Wouldn't sound as good on the operation reports," Tareau said gloomily. "And we're going to have to write them about those hills."

So Reno, Carson and Vegas it was.

Looking out at the outposts, Caputo and Tareau didn't like the odds. Reno, the farthest away, rose some 1350 meters from the Marine lines, much of the way to it under enemy observation and fire. Behind Reno, and, not quite so exposed, Carson and Vegas were lower and easier to reach, and they could support Reno by fire.

It was hard to get to Reno. The Korean Service Corps laborers had had to dig a trench across the saddles to reach it at all — a monumental tunneling operation. Relief and resupply had to be at night, or not at all. And once on the outpost hill, Marines could only dig in on the reverse slopes.

Higher ground held by the enemy looked right down Reno's throat. The front slope of the hill was untenable. But on the rear, the garrison dug living bunkers connected by a deep fighting trench from which they could fire at attackers coming across the crest or around the sides of Reno.

The reason Caputo and Tareau bucked the odds was simple; Reno loomed over a large part of the Marine MLR. In American hands, it was no threat to the CCF — but if the Chinks had it, they dominated both Carson and Vegas and could bring direct fire on a large section of the main line. They could make life completely miserable for Marines holding the gateway to Seoul.

Colonel Caputo and Major Tareau did what they could to copper their bet and lower the odds. They sent machine guns and tons of ammo up to Reno. They coordinated fires of the mortars, artillery, tanks and forward companies to box in all approaches to the hill. They asked for and got an Army Searchlight Detachment to stand ready to illuminate the outpost on call. They set up a plan by which a platoon of Dog Company would make a diversionary attack on a Chink outpost if the pressure on Reno grew too great.

And they knew how the Chink operators liked to deal their cards — Old Joe preferred to slip troops past an outpost, surround it and cut it off before swamping it.

To circumvent such a move, 2nd Battalion each night sent a blocking force — one platoon — to take up positions behind Reno where they could support by fire, reinforce or halt possible enemy encirclement. The platoon went out after dark and came back prior to dawn. 2nd Battalion wanted to play this one close to its chest, not let Joe guess what it had up its sleeve.

But it could only place some thirty-six Marines on Reno. There simply wasn't room for more than that. Realistically, the C.O. and Operations Officer drew up a plan whereby all local fires could be brought down on Reno itself if the Chinese ever got into its defenses.

As the nights grew cold and the days turned crisp in the rolling brown hills of the Injin Valley, the Marines put on their field jackets and waited for the action to get hot.

Old Joe Chink, they knew, was a gambler, too.

At dusk October 26, 1952, Major Mack Tareau invited his friend, Major Shelley, for dinner at his club, and they left the operations bunker in the capable hands of Gunnery Sergeant Bullenthrush, a scarred, old China hand in his forties.

Bullenthrush had been a temporary officer in the Big War, and he was a stout, well-built NCO who could run the CP with no sweat.

Joe Shelley ran the Weapons Company. A dark, crew-cut ex-enlisted Marine, he had been a demolitions man in the Pacific and had developed a kind of flinch upon hearing loud noises. Because of a prominent terrain feature in the center of his visage, he was known — not universally, but by majors and above — as "Hose Nose."

He looked at the creamed corned beef in his tin mess plate and remarked, "Mack, you really must have dinner at *my* club tomorrow."

Mack, tall and dark and very slim, grinned under his thick eyebrows as he pushed his plate back. "Done."

They walked back to the Operations bunker, feeling the snap in the air. Inside the bunker Bullenthrush stood up to greet them.

"Anything new, Gunny?"

"Quiet, sir."

Tareau got on the horn, held a conference call with the company skippers. He took the day's action reports, coordinated patrols and other routine matters. The info came in in code over the wire.

"Ho, ho," Hose Nose muttered. "Another night, like any other night."

"Another day, another dollar, sir," Bullenthrush said.

But it was not to be another night like any other night. At 0040, forty minutes past midnight, Joe started to roll the dice.

At 0035, on Reno, Private Edwin Crutchley's job was to stand guard in the trenchworks, which task he regarded with a certain lack of enthusiasm since it came with clockwork regularity each night, and demanded very little skill.

Still, peering into the dark with alert brown eyes, Crutchley was not apt to slough off — not with his tail more than one thousand yards out in front of friendly lines.

Slap-slap-slap-slap. The noise sounded like a lot of hands slapping on gunstocks, in time. And it came from over the crest of the hill in the direction of the Chink lines.

He figured he'd better get the platoon sergeant up. But he was spared that chore, for suddenly somebody out in the dark put mouth to whistle and screeched a loud blast.

Firing, hurling grenades and yelling, a wave of Chinese burst over the crest of Reno. Amid the fiendish racket a second wave lashed at the trench from the right.

The darkness came apart in gun flashes, screams and the crump, of grenades.

Captain Flores, skipper of Easy Company, whose men were out on Reno, was on the hot line to Battalion. There was a hint of worry in the New Mexican's voice: "Reno's been hit again!"

At the other end of the field wire Major Tareau said, "We can hear it." The racket of bugles and horns carried clearly through the crisp night. Tareau had no direct wire to Reno; communication with the outpost had to come through Easy. "What are you up against?"

"Don't know yet. No word from Reno. All we can hear is the damn bugles and shooting."

"Keep us informed, Rudy."

"Right, soon as I know," Flores said.

Along the communications trench leading out to Reno, Sergeant Bruno Kopperman heard the bugles, too. And then his blocking platoon, two squads left of the ditch and one on the right, was ass-deep in Chinks.

It was hard to say who was more surprised, the Chinks or the tall, blond platoon sergeant. In a wild melee, the right-hand squad was overrun despite its light Browning machine gun.

Marines and Chinese fired at each other at pointblank range. Kopperman yelled at his second squad to move across the trench to give the hard-hit squad a hand.

As the squad tried to cross the ditch, heavy mortar and artillery fire came down on them from the enemy lines.

Bram! Bram!

But the same fire came down on the Chinks, knocking them sprawling. Kopperman's men moved in grimly, firing rifles and Thompsons. The Chinks tossed back grenades. For a minute or two a wild fire fight blazed along the trench.

Half of Kopperman's men were down, killed or wounded. But there was no question of who was ahead as the Chinks fled back into the darkness to the right of Reno.

The right side of the trench showed a few dead Marines. But it was littered with Chinese in cotton uniforms and soft caps.

A few more Chinks got into the trench, tried running down it. The Marine M-1s cut them down before they were within bayonet reach.

Kopperman's platoon had taken its losses, but its job was done.

Out on Reno the machine guns chopped away at the Chinese waves whipping across the hill. All four had begun firing at once as the Chinks came over the crest.

But the Chinks coming over the hill carried bags of grenades, and they tossed them with both hands. A long, black potato masher bounced off a machine gun barrel, lay smoking. Private Ed Crutchley saw it blow up suddenly, putting the machine gun crew out of action with wounds.

Savagely he let go with his rifle, saw a big Chink grab his stomach, fall tumbling into the trench. *Damn, that one was close!* Ed knew that if the Chinks ever got into the trench system Reno was in trouble.

More grenades blasted a second machine gun crew back away from its weapon. The long, black sticks flew out of the night in a constant stream, blowing smoke and dirt everywhere.

Edson, the rough little platoon sergeant, came running down the firing trench. "Get some men on those guns!" he shouted.

Sergeant Edson was a rough, tough little guy, the kind apt to get in trouble in the rear areas. But on the firing line he was superb — and when he had asked for a second tour on Reno, he'd got it.

It was one way to keep Edson out of trouble. The kind of trouble he was in now he thrived on.

Crutchley and two of the other riflemen put down their M-1s and jumped on the Browning light MGs. Soon the guns were once again hammering at the Chinese waves coming over the crest of Reno.

The second wave of Chinks carried no grenades, only blazing burp guns. They ran into the orange-purple flashes of the machine guns, wavered and fell away.

Within ten minutes it was all over. First Lieutenant James Roy was surprised to find his wire still in to Easy Company. As the firing died away, and even the Marine mortar and artillery barrages around Reno slackened, the officer in charge of Reno was reporting in. He was a big, well-built young man, brown-haired, calm-voiced.

He told Rudy Flores, "Skipper, I've lost six-eight men, killed or WIA. But they never got in the trenches — " Roy was well aware that Chinks inside the defense system in the dark could play hell with holding the hill. "But it's not over. We can hear 'em talking on the front slope, carting off their wounded."

"We'll put fire on them," Flores promised. "Hang on!"

During the lull, while Marine supporting weapons blazed away at the sounds of Chinese movement, Roy brought his wounded inside and resupplied his men with ammo. The more lightly wounded men were set to loading BAR and carbine magazines.

Everybody knew Old Joe still held the dice and another pass was coming up.

At Battalion, when the shooting started, Mack Tareau snapped at Bullenthrush, "Go get the Colonel!"

A few seconds later Caputo dashed in, carrying his boots in his hand. "What the hell's up?"

Hand on the map board, Tareau briefed him.

Then Major Tareau got Captain Ed Wilcox who was standing by the hot loop. Wilcox's Dog Company was selected to furnish the platoon which would make the diversionary action if things got out of hand.

"Ed, you want a piece of the action?"

"Hell, yes!"

"Start moving your men onto Carson."

Then he had Captain Rodney's Headquarters and Service Company on the wire. H & S was ordered to ready two provisional platoons of cooks, clerks and drivers — Headquarters pogues — to move up on the line if needed.

He had more to do. No one was supposed to talk about it — by order — but there was something called an ammunition shortage in Korea. Tareau called up his friend who was ammunition officer on Division staff. "Look, Bullets old boy, we got troubles. Are you going to give us a hard time if we shoot up a few 81s and four-point-deuces?"

Bullets allowed that if shooting them would save old Mack's tail, he would not.

Tareau alerted four tanks to move into position to support Reno. He asked the Artillery liaison officer to get word to the Army Searchlight team to stand ready in case they were needed.

At 0105, the second Chinese assault boiled up over Reno. A screeching wave came over the crest while a second washed around the flank of the hill and charged in from the right.

"Them guys are in a rut," Private Crutchley said. Nobody took time to laugh. Maybe they didn't think it was funny.

In the operations bunker Colonel Caputo slammed his hand down on the map table, indicating to the artillery liaison people where he wanted fires. "Box 'em! Fire the box!

The pounding shook Hose Nose Shelley awake. An old battle hand, he had dozed off. Shaking his head, he assembled the weapons company fires as directed. Marine artillery and mortars boxed Reno in a wall of fire and whining metal.

On Reno, once again the assaulting Chinks ran into the machine guns. For a few minutes it was touch and go. *My God*, Crutchley thought, seeing a knot of Chinks trying to run into the trenches with a load of planks, *They've come to stay. They're bringing lumber with 'em!"*

He swiveled the gun, tripped the firing studs again. The gun yammered, cutting through boards and flesh. *What the hell are they goin' to build up here — a craphouse?*

Then, suddenly as it had come, the attack melted away. Dead and dying Chinese were now piled in windrows all about the entrenchments on Reno.

Lieutenant Roy tried the phone. It was dead. One of the wounded men tended the radio; now he broke listening silence. He might tell the Chink something over the air, but Battalion had to know, too.

"We're still in good shape," he said confidently. "I've got four or five killed, the rest wounded. We've got ammo up the gazoo. Hell, we're in good shape!"

Outside in the darkness Roy could hear Chinese groaning and crying on the ground. It wasn't like the Chinks to leave their own behind — they swept the battlefield when they could.

The outpost had seen them this time — now it was their turn to call.

At 0400, a Chinese battalion did the calling. They blew their horns, they tooted their bugles. Then they whiplashed into the beleaguered outpost once again.

In the operations bunker Major Shelley said explosively, "Shithouse mouse!"

Weakly, the radio came into Battalion from deep in the bowels of the Reno trenches: "They're coming in on top of us — waves of 'em — can't stop 'em — "

Wounded, Lieutenant Roy didn't have time to talk to Battalion. He joined in the fire fight. Edson was hit, but stayed on his feet. Crutchley was hit. *Hell, everybody was hit.*

They kept fighting, hosing the oncoming groups of Chinks with lead. It was like Hallowe'en. The Chinese blew horns, whirled noise makers that sounded like snapping sticks. They threw grenades and fired burp guns. They never stopped coming. And they died.

"Get the fire in! Shelley, move that fire in!" Colonel Caputo kept saying in a certain agony.

Every supporting weapon in the Battalion moved its sights onto the slopes of Reno. They belched fire and lead and explosives.

On Reno a few Chinks got into the trenches. Crutchley couldn't train the MG on them. Sweating with exertion, he grabbed up a bunker bomb — an 81mm mortar shell container filled with napalm, with a white phosphorus grenade for trigger — and threw it.

Blooom!

Spattered with napalm, burning at 3,000 degrees Fahrenheit, a Chink ran squalling into the night.

In the operations bunker Mack Tareau called for the Army to put the searchlights on the hill. It took four minutes to pass the word.

Then in a blaze of glory the violent bright beams cut through the dark. Millions of candlepower sliced into the smoke and haze over Reno, barely outlining the hill. Back at battalion the staff officers peered out toward the fire-streaked acre of fury that still smoked and racketed in the night.

There were Chinks all over the hill — like black flies on a dead carcass.

"Who's got it — them or us?" Tareau asked, sweating.

"No bet," Shelley muttered.

Mack looked at Colonel Caputo. "I think we ought to fire everything we've got on the hill!" He turned to the radio man "Tell Roy to pull his head down."

Caputo looked at the artillery liaison. "Pull the goddamn plug!"

They pulled it. For ten minutes it sounded like real war, not Truman's police action. Everything Battalion had, plus Division artillery, slammed directly into Reno.

I hope our Marines are deep, Tareau thought.

When it came in, the radio from Reno was very faint. They had taken it deep in the bunker. *We're still holding. Chinks piled up everywhere — VT fires caught 'em in open.* Then, *they're pulling back — they're pulling off!*

Mack and Shelley and Colonel Caputo went outside the bunker, past the big sign they had put up there: KILL THE COMMUNIST BASTARDS. It was the beginning of morning nautical twilight — a faint gray light revealed the hill shadows. On Reno smoke was blowing away.

The Chinese were gone. They knew snake eyes when they saw 'em.

Caputo said, "Put some Willie Peter — white phosphorus — on the hill. Smoke it so Roy can get his casualties out."

"Yes, sir."

"Tell Flores to relieve him with another platoon."

"Yes, sir."

On Reno the six Marines still on their feet were rolling Chinese bodies out of their trenches and living bunkers. Among the six were Roy, Edson and Edwin Crutchley.

In the operations bunker Shelley said, "Breakfast at my club?"

"You're on."

Shelley yawned. "Aw, hell," he said tiredly. "A day like any other day — "

"Another day, another dollar, sir," Bullenthrush said as they went to breakfast.

It was like that in Korea. Sometimes you won, sometimes you lost. And once in a while a long shot paid off — as on Reno.

In Koreas by 1953 the Old Breed was almost gone. However, a new-old breed had taken over, and they were doing very well.

In July 1953 the fighting in Korea came to an end. It was called "cease-fire": no peace treaty or permanent settlement to the war has yet been signed. The Marines were subsequently withdrawn, leaving Army and South Korean troops to hold the cease-fire line. These remain on watch along an uneasy, fortified demarcation area. However, Marines now afloat and at Camp Pendleton, California, including reservists, stand ready for rapid deployment in Asia if the call should come. The world is still a dangerous place; the nation still needs Marines. Aboard far-flung Navy fleets, at bases at home and abroad, the Corps prepared for that call.

Inevitably, with the passage of time many things have changed. Many women now serve in the Corps, although not in ground combat jobs. The names and faces change. There are Americans in the ranks whose fathers were not born when Guadalcanal was fought, men not born when their fathers fought in Vietnam. Weapons and equipment change from decade to decade.

The training, discipline, and pride does not change.

The Corps has fought in twelve major conflicts and more than two hundred lesser-intensity campaigns. The Corps is actually older than our nation, and in over two hundred and twenty five years it became one of the most spectacular fighting forces the world has seen. Its deeds are legend. More important, its deeds are fact. They form a vital part of American history.

The name of Belleau Wood, Tarawa, and Chosin should be remembered with pride. Those now unborn hopefully, will hear of them. Their story has been told before and will be told again. But, these tales must be told again and again, so that the nameless, formless youth that don Marine green knows what it means, and what they must become, to bear the title, United States Marine.

After two centuries the mold is set, and it is a good one.

The years, peaceful or bloody, will pass; times and faces will change again. The Old Corps, as always gives way to the new.

But Americans must never allow the breed to change.

About the Author

During World War II, the late Fehrenbach served with the US Infantry and Engineers as platoon sergeant with an engineer battalion. He continued his military career in the Korean War, rising from platoon leader to company commander and then to battalion staff officer of the 72nd Tank battalion, 2nd Infantry Division. Prior to his military involvement, a young T. R. Fehrenbach, born in San Benito, Texas, worked as a farmer and the owner of an insurance company. His most enduring work is *Lone Star*, a one-volume history of Texas. In retirement, he wrote a political column for a San Antonio newspaper. He sold numerous pieces to publications such as the *Saturday Evening Post* and *Argosy*. He is author of several books, including *U.S. Marines in Action*, *The Battle of Anzio*, and *This Kind of War*.

Open Road Integrated Media is a digital publisher and multimedia content company. Open Road creates connections between authors and their audiences by marketing its ebooks through a new proprietary online platform, which uses premium video content and social media.

Videos, Archival Documents, and New Releases

Sign up for the Open Road Media newsletter and get news delivered straight to your inbox.

Sign up now at
www.openroadmedia.com/newsletters

FIND OUT MORE AT
WWW.OPENROADMEDIA.COM

FOLLOW US:
@openroadmedia and
Facebook.com/OpenRoadMedia